J.

£3.00

Phantasmagrams

Phantasmagrams

A collection of visual and optical illusions designed by Pentagram

EBURY PRESS · LONDON

Published in 1992 by Ebury Press
an imprint of the Random Century Group
Random Century House
20 Vauxhall Bridge Road
London SW1V 2SA

Design by David Hillman, Pentagram Design
Akio Morishima
Text by David Gibbs

A catalogue record for this book is available from the British Library.

ISBN 0 09 177041 6

Printed in Singapore by Tien Wah Press

When you know how the magic works,
you cast the spell that brings a smile of mystification.
When you don't know the sleight of hand,
the trick of the eye, beware;
what you see is what you don't get.

THE HEXACUBE

See it one way and it's a
hexagon. See it another way
and it's a cube in perspective.

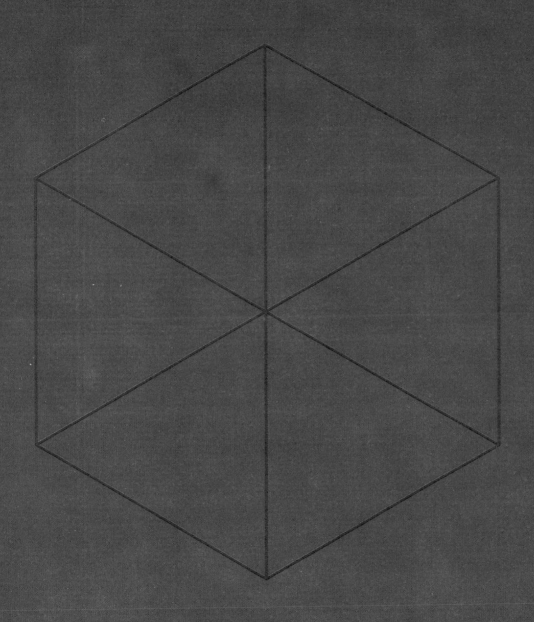

CHANGING SHAPE

Hold the page away from you
and the round shapes begin
to look like hexagons.

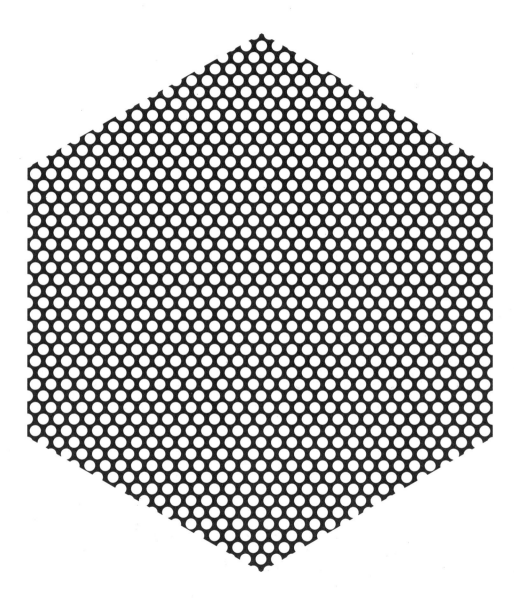

FRENCH DROP

This is a basic trick well known to magicians; it is useful as a part of all sorts of other tricks. You hold a coin by its edges in your left hand between finger and thumb. Move your right hand, palm down, over the left as if it were going to take the coin. As the coin is hidden by the fingers of the right hand, release it and let it fall back into the left hand so that it comes to rest in the palm. It can be adjusted or pressed here momentarily by the left thumb. By clenching the right hand at the same time it looks as though you have passed the coin from one hand to the other. With the coin 'palmed' in the left hand you can open both hands with backs towards the audience. Look, no coin.

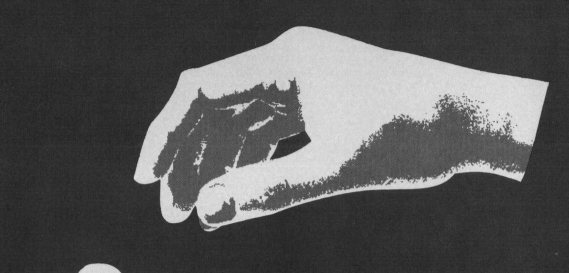

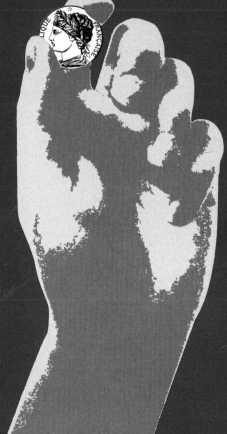

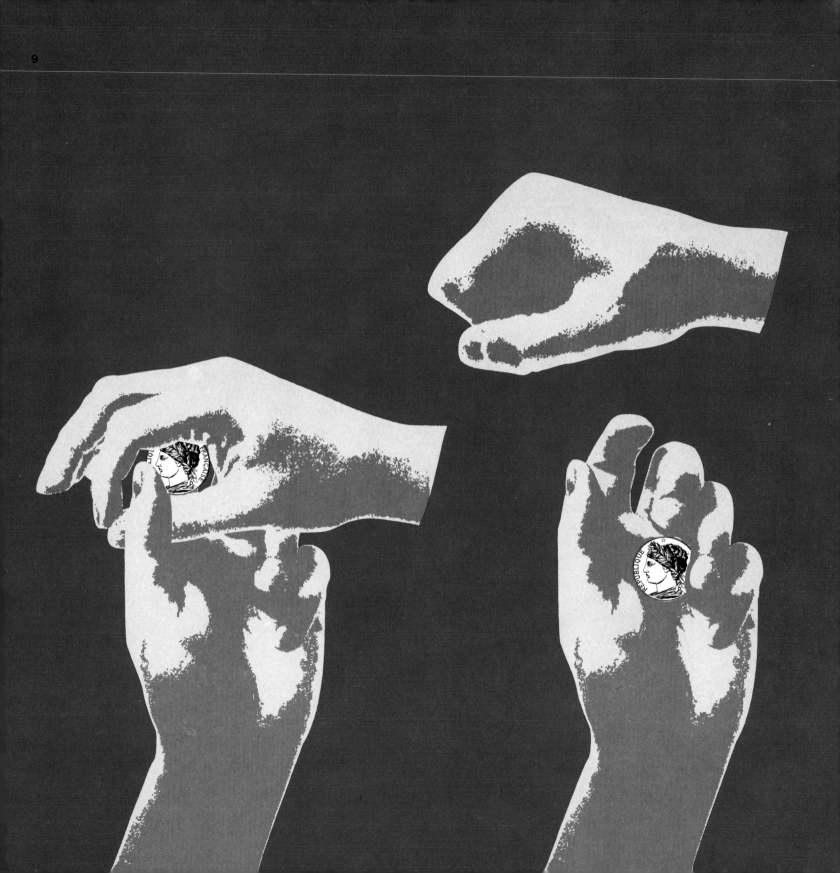

TRAP THE RIBBON

You need a pencil and a length of stiff ribbon (a strap or belt will do just as well). Loop the ribbon in half. Roll it neatly from the centre and place it on the table. Ask a spectator to insert a pencil in the loop at the centre of the coil and hold it firmly against the table. Holding both ends, pull the ribbon straight and it will be caught by the pencil in the loop. Now you can challenge the spectator to try again. Wherever he tries to place the pencil, it will never catch the ribbon in the loop again.

This is what you do. When you double the ribbon into the loop make sure that one end is a little longer. Roll it up from the centre until the first end is reached. Hold it in place by your forefinger and lay the coil it on the table. Now ask the spectator to insert the pencil again. If he places the pencil wrongly in the 'green' position shown, unravel the coil holding the ends of the ribbon - at the points marked 'green'. If the spectator places the pencil correctly in the 'red' position shown, unravel the coil by holding the ribbon at points marked 'red'. If you do this right the ribbon will never end up trapped by the pencil.

SPINNING SPIRALS

Rotate the page one way and the spirals seem to expand; the other way and they contract.

THE BORING FIGURE

Here is an old lady. Here is also a young girl. If you can't see them both, try making the young girl's chin the nose of the old lady. Got it? This was first published in 1915, drawn by W E Hill, and became known as the Boring Figure.

15

PARTIAL IMMUNITY

Place a mirror on the line at right angles to the page and look at the reflection of the words. Some change, some don't. The reason is that some letters are so formed that upside down they are mirror images of themselves. Thus looking at them upside down in a mirror they appear normal.

CHOICE	PURPLE	HIDE
SLEEP	DIED	TIGER
ICE BOX	SQUARE	ECHO
TURTLE	COOKBOOK	LARGE
OBOE	ROSE	CHECKED
WATER	DECIDED	TABLE

MAKE YOUR OWN ANAMORPHOSIS

An anamorphosis is the name of the specially distorted image that can only be revealed by viewing it in a tube mirror. You will find a number of anamorphoses in this book. To make your own, draw your object on a grid, or place a grid on a photograph or illustration. Carefully copy the image on to the anamorphosis grid square by square. Roll the flexible mirror that comes with this book into a tube. Place it at the centre of arc made by the anamorphosis and see the image brought back to normal by viewing it in your tube mirror.

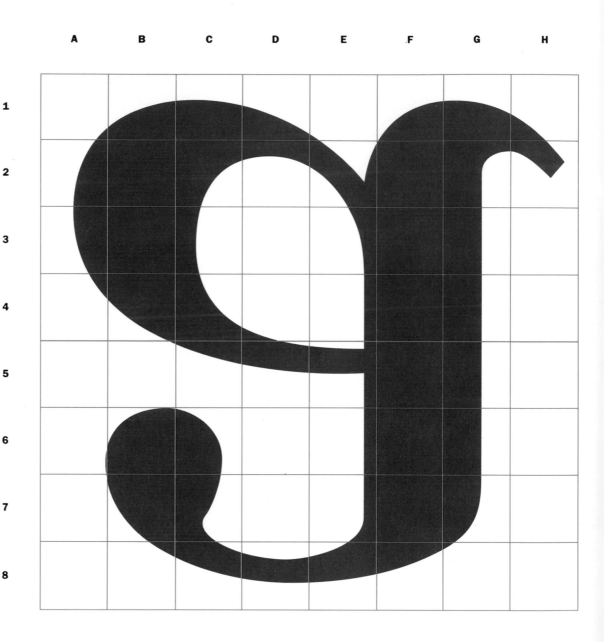

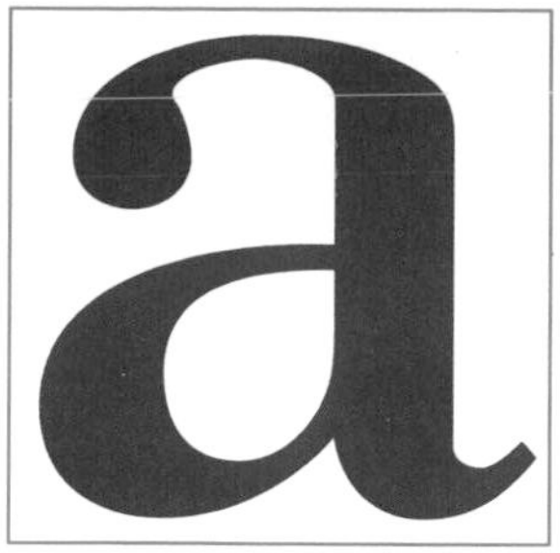

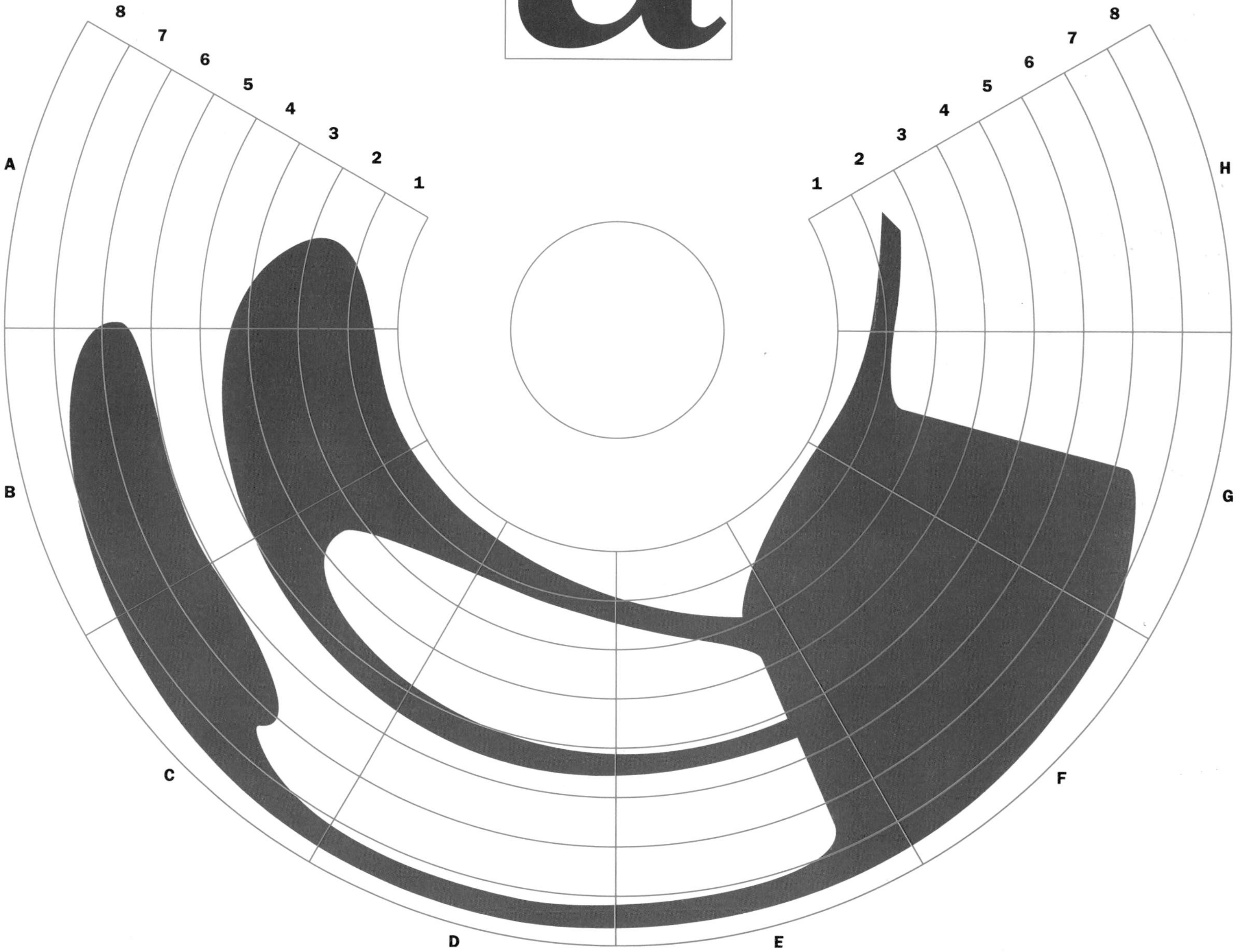
8
7
6
5
4
3
2
1
A
B
C
D
E
F
G
H
1
2
3
4
5
6
7
8

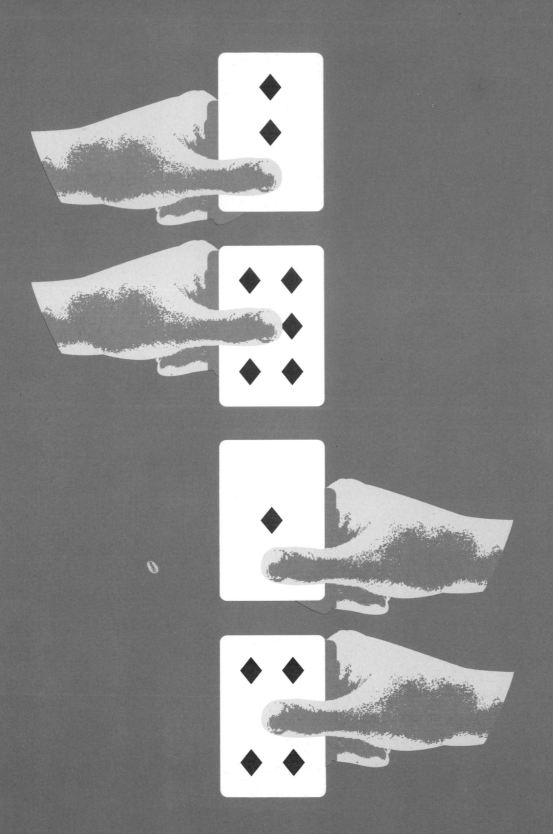

THE FOUR-SIDED CARD

You have to make your
own playing card for this;
diamonds are easiest
to draw. Follow the
arrangements shown below,
one on each side of the card.
Now by the judicious
placement of the thumb you
can fool the audience into
thinking you are holding
either the six of diamonds,
the three, the four or the ace.

MOUNTED UP

It seems just a jumble of patches at first. But try turning the page anti-clockwise through 90° - then you'll see somebody being taken for a ride.

GHOSTS

Do you see those grey shady spots on the white lines at the corners of the boxes? Try catching one by looking at it directly. It's not there.

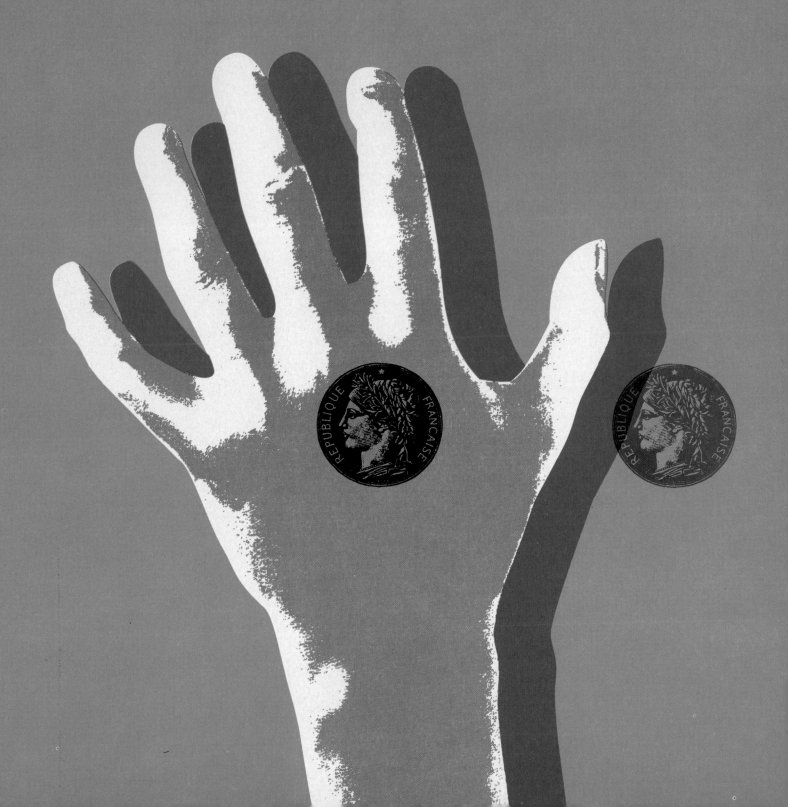

YOU NEVER LOSE

Which hand is the coin under? Whichever hand is chosen, it will always be under the other. This is how you do it. Hold a coin in your right palm at the base of the two middle fingers. (Left-handed people may find it's easier with the coin in the left hand.) Slap both your hands down on to a table, which must be smooth and shiny. Ask your spectator which hand the coin is under. If the correct hand is chosen, flip it over with a sharp flick of the wrist, keeping the palm flat and pushing down on the coin. This will make the coin shoot out sideways. If you raise the other hand slightly the coin will slide under it. Get the action right and the coin will move so fast it will not be noticed. You could make your fortune like this.

MAGIC MIRROR PICTURE

Roll the flexible mirror that comes with this book into a tube. Place the tube on the circle of the anamorphosis - the name for this specially distorted picture - and it will reveal its hidden reality in the tube mirror. The picture is called *Man with Wine Glass and Flask*, an original anamorphosis from the Gold Collection of Toys at the Museum of the City of New York.

BEARDED WONDER

This is not just a jumble of splodges. It's a picture of a bearded man. Keep looking.

I
LOVE
PARIS IN THE
THE SPRINGTIME

There's nothing wrong with
the drawing as such, although
the object could not exist.

COIN DISPENSER

Sitting at a table across from your audience, lay a handkerchief on the table in front of you, with one corner draping over the edge. Place a coin at the centre of the handkerchief and fold it in. Pick up the handkerchief as if you were holding it by the hidden coin, but secretly let the coin fall into your lap. Now shake open the handkerchief and the coin vanishes into thin air. This trick is particularly rewarding if you use other people's money.

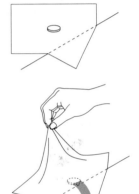

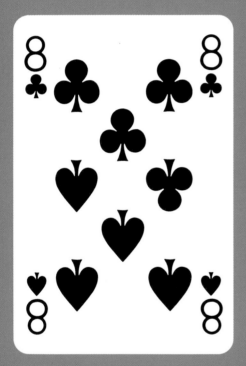

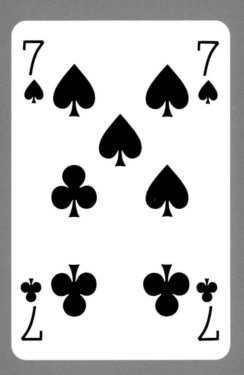

STICKY FINGERS

Ask someone to push two cards into the middle of a pack. You then throw the pack on to the table - and the two cards remain in your hand. The trick depends on fooling the memory. Before starting, place the seven of clubs on the bottom of the pack and the eight of spades on the top. Look through the pack and find the seven of spades and the eight of clubs. Give them to your spectator and ask him to put them into the pack anywhere he likes. Square off the pack to reassure your audience that the two cards are well and truly lost.

Now hold the pack firmly with your fingers on the top and thumb on the bottom. Throw the pack down while squeezing on the top and bottom cards. The two cards will stay in your hand while the rest of the pack falls on to the table. Reveal the cards in your hand and the spectator will believe they are the ones buried in the pack. The fact that you are showing the seven of spades and eight of clubs rather than the seven of clubs and eight of spades never seems to be noticed.

The thicker horizontal lines are straight. It's your eyes playing you up again.

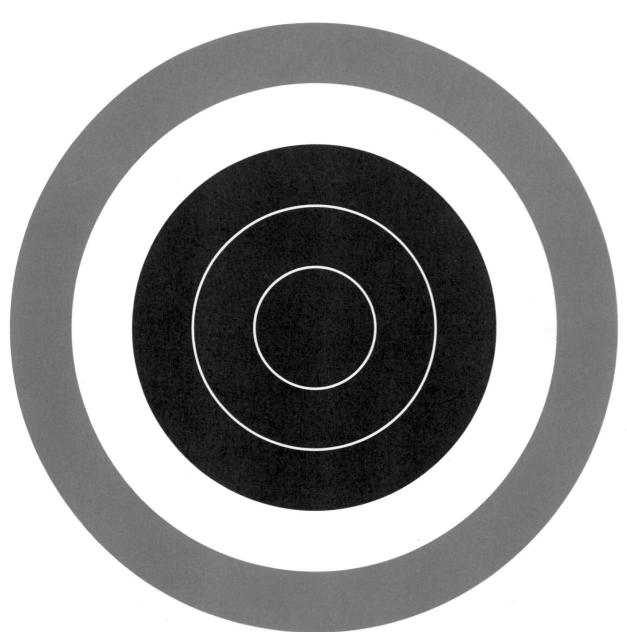

GOING ROUND IN CIRCLES

Just by looking, you would think that the shaded inner bands together have a greater area than the shaded outer band. Wrong; they are both the same.

For geometricians, here's the proof: Take the radius of the whole circle as 5. Then the inner radius of the shaded outer band is 4, and the radius of the central shaded area is 3. Thus the area of the shaded outer band is $\pi r^2 = \pi \times 3^2 = 9\pi$ square units. And the area of the central shaded area is $(\pi \times 5^2) - (\pi \times 4^2) = 25\pi - 16\pi = 9\pi$ square units.

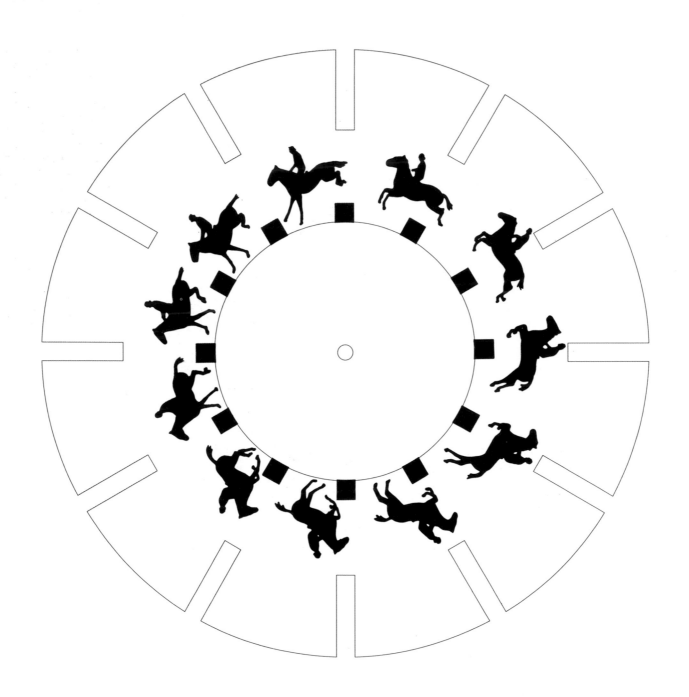

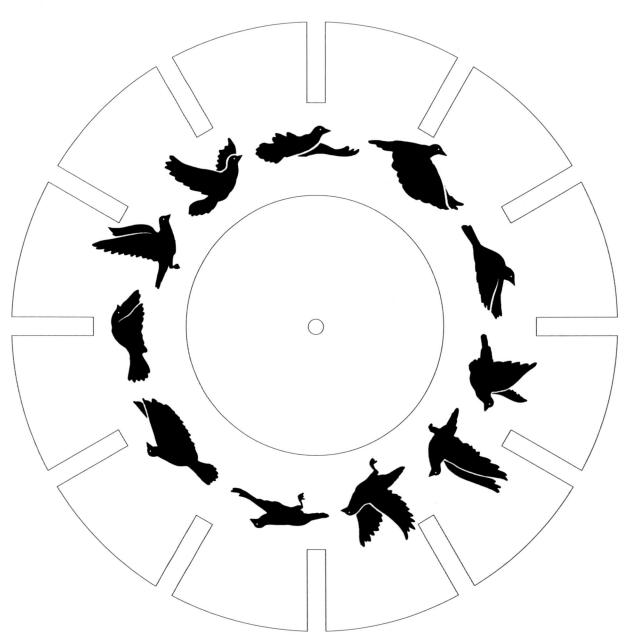

THE KINEMATOSCOPE

If you go to the movies, what you see is really an illusion - the film is just a series of still pictures. These kinematograph discs work on the same principle. Take photocopies of the discs, mount them on card and cut them out carefully, including the slots. Stick a drawing pin through the card from the front and into a stick at the back, so that you can twirl the disc. Look through the slots at the reflection of the card in the mirror as you twirl it. Things start to move.

Which pencil is the longer?
Which is the shorter? Neither
is either.

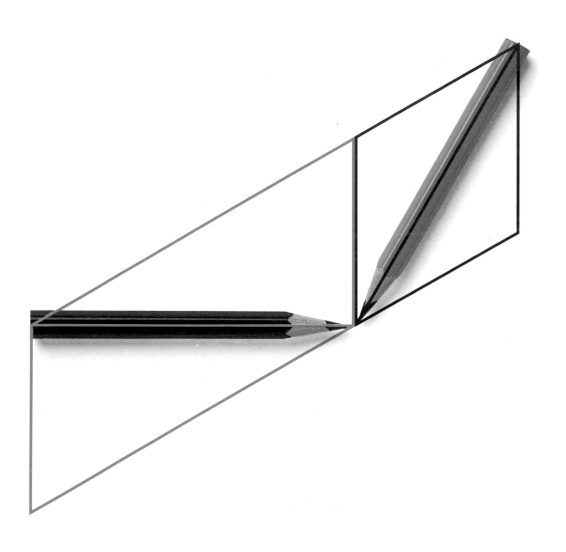

MORE EQUAL

The bottom shape may look bigger, but they are both exactly the same size and shape.

ANCIENT ANAMORPHOSIS

Saint Jerome Praying is a seventeenth-century oil painting, presently in the Centraal Museum, Utrecht. It is by one of the followers of Caravaggio, many of whom favoured the anamorphosis representation of subjects. Roll the flexible mirror that comes with this book into a tube. Place it in the centre of the arc made by the picture and see the wonderful detail revealed.

38

EYE BOREDOM

The pattern here is uniform and regular. Yet when you look at it the restless eye tries to make patterns within the pattern, as if it could not accept there is nothing here but sameness.

SHE'S NO SQUARE

Someone's laughing at you...

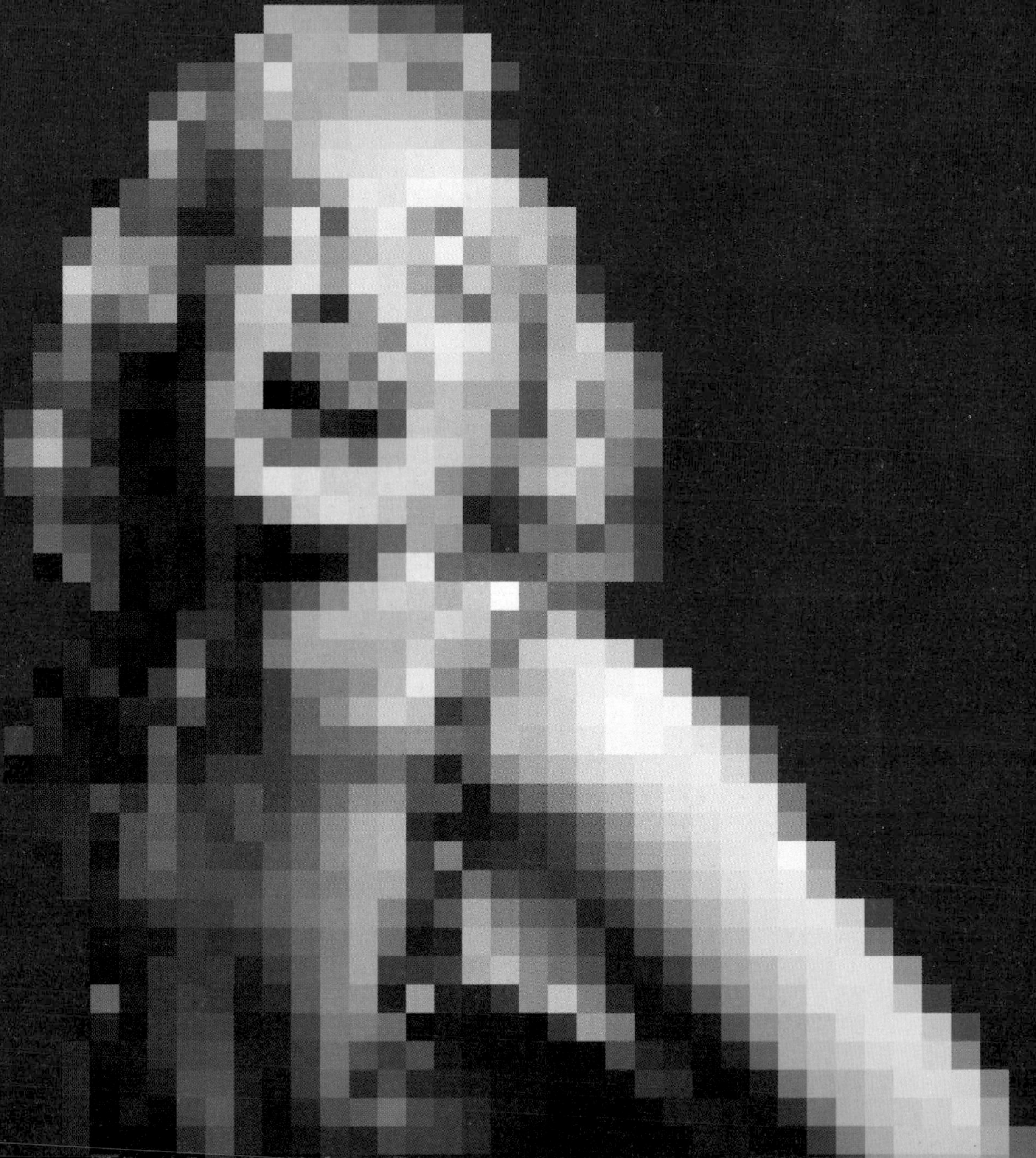

DOUBLE YOUR MONEY

You can appear to be twice as well off, with this clever piece of folding. Lay a bill or note flat. Following the diagram, fold X to X and Z to Z away from you. Now fold the lines A to A and B to B towards you. Press point A to the right and the corresponding fold at the back to the left. How much are you worth now?

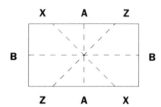

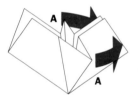

MEND YOUR BROKEN HEART

Place a card vertically between the two halves of the broken heart. Move your face towards it so the right eye only sees the right half of the heart, and the left eye the left half. The two halves will appear to join together.

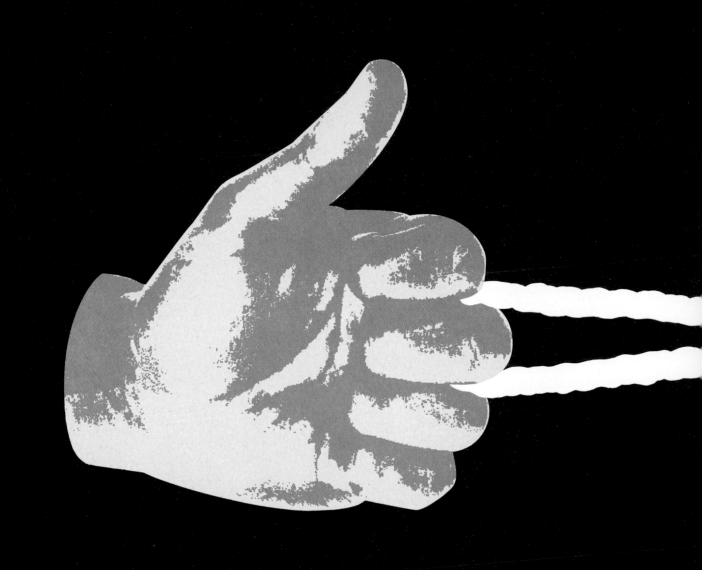

44

HIDDEN MEANING

There is a word hidden in this pattern. Keep looking and you should be able to figure it out.

LINE UP

Which of the two lines
continues to the single line?
Take your bets before
checking.

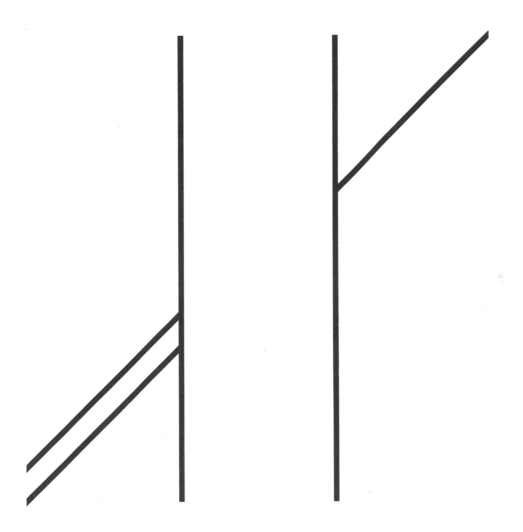

FORCING A CARD

This is the basis for many a good card trick - like the one opposite. You ask someone to pick a card as you riffle through the pack. You can tell him what the card is without appearing to see the card yourself.

Here's how. Place the card you want chosen on top of the pack. Riffle through the cards with your right hand by placing your fingers at the front of the pack and your thumb at the back. Ask someone to tell you when to stop, and then lift the top part of the pack with your right hand as if opening a book. At the same time push down on the top card with the fingers of your left hand, as shown.

Now pull away with your right hand, letting the top card slide onto the cards remaining in your left hand - all in one swift motion. The spectator then takes the forced card, imagining it to have been at the place in the pack where you were asked to stop. Of course, you know what it is.

SURE SHOT

Someone chooses a card. You ask them to 'shoot' it while in the pack - and out it pops, bullet hole and all. For this you will need a pack of cards and one extra card from an identical pack. Make a 'bullet' hole through the duplicate card - for added realism you can even carefully burn the edges of the hole with a match. Put a rubber band around the card and place it in the pack near the bottom. Place the identical card on top of the pack.

Now 'force' the identical card as described opposite and have it returned to the pack. Cut the pack so that the 'bullet' card with a rubber band around it is roughly in the middle. Explain that you are going to put a rubber band around the whole pack and pretend to search for one in your pocket. Taking your hand out of your pocket, move it quickly towards the pack held in your other hand. Now grab the rubber band around the card and pull it up over the rest of the pack, as shown - it will look as if you have simply put a rubber band around the pack, like you said.

Ask someone to point his fingers pistol-fashion at the pack and say: 'Bang!' As you slacken your grip on the pack, the card you prepared with a bullet hole will fly up out of the pack.

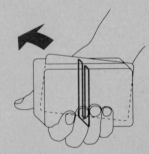

Do you first see the arrows pointing to the left, or the ones pointing to the right? If you come across this on a highway, turn the car round and go home.

Vigorously rotate the page in a small circle; the six wheels will appear to revolve independently, with the central cog turning in the opposite direction.

WARP FACTOR

Which one of these two dots is the real centre of the circle? The one on the left is. The other seems to be the correct one because the arcs are warping your perception.

BENHAM'S COLOUR TOP

Make a disc of cardboard, 5 inches in diameter. Mark it out in solid black as shown, or you can take a photocopy of the pattern, cut it out and glue it to the card. Make a hole in the centre and push a pencil through so that the disc will spin.

Colours will appear out of the spinning black-and-white disc. The effect may vary for different people, but spun clockwise the inner band usually shows red, the next band green, the next yellow and the outer blue. Spun anti-clockwise, you may see blue on the inner, then yellow, then green and red on the outer.

THE FRASER SPIRAL

The illusion is of a spiral descending into infinity. Look again. The spiral is actually a number of circles going nowhere. Fraser was the fellow who invented this twisted cord trick-of-the-eye in 1908.

WINE TO WATER

Change the contents of the glass from dark red wine to white wine, and then to water. Choose a wine glass that widens towards the top, or at least has straight sides. The illusion is achieved by placing two pieces of glass or transparent plastic cut to fit the wine glass as vertical partitions. One of the pieces should be pale sherry colour; the other, cut slightly taller, should be ruby red.

Fill the glass with water, place the two partitions in it, one against the other, and the liquid will turn dark red. Show it to the audience with the partitions facing them, and declare it to be a glass of red wine. Now place a handkerchief over the glass. Accompanied by suitable magic words, nip the taller of the two partitions and whisk it away under the handkerchief. The red wine has turned to white wine. Repeat the process nipping away the second partition, and the wine has turned to water. Not exactly a miracle, but enough to puzzle the audience a while.

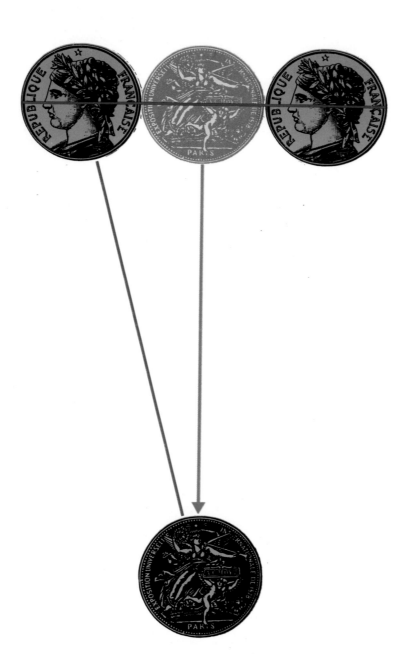

Take three coins and place them in a row. Slide the centre coin straight downward and stop it where you think that the distance between it and either of the remaining coins equals the distance between the outside edges of the remaining coins. People invariably place the middle coin too close to the other coins. It's much further than you think - you'll need a ruler to believe just how much.

A THIRD EXTRA

Place two large coins between your fingers. Rub the coins together with quick short up-and-down strokes. Watch closely; there appears to be a third coin between the original two.

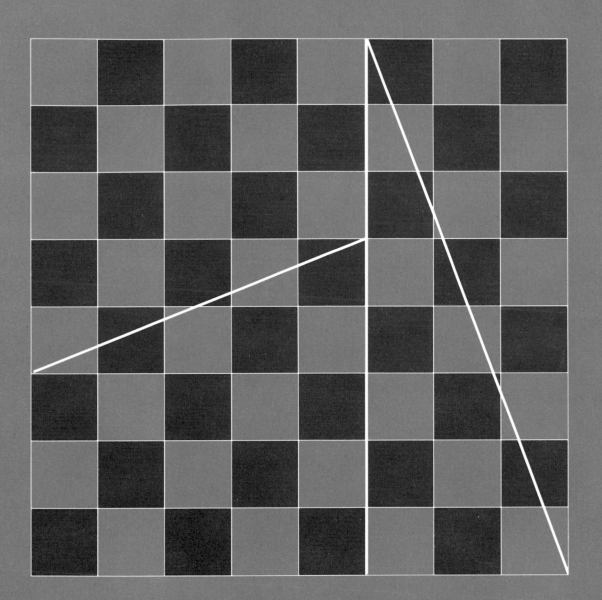

SQUARE CREATION

Witness the creation of a square from nothing. There are 64 squares (8 x 8) in the large square. If you cut it up along the lines and reassemble it as in the diagram there are 65 squares (5 x 13). But the areas have to be the same. So where did the extra square come from?

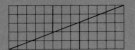

CUTE COMPENSATION

Gaze at the mouth of Marilyn on the left under good light for twenty seconds or so. Quickly shift to Marilyn's mouth on the right. She blushes prettily and her background turns blue. This is not the effect of your personality, but your eyes compensating for seeing too much of the same colour - blue being the complementary colour to red.

Follow this step-by-step knot diagram, and end up with nothing. Its main use is for tying up prisoners you think are innocent.

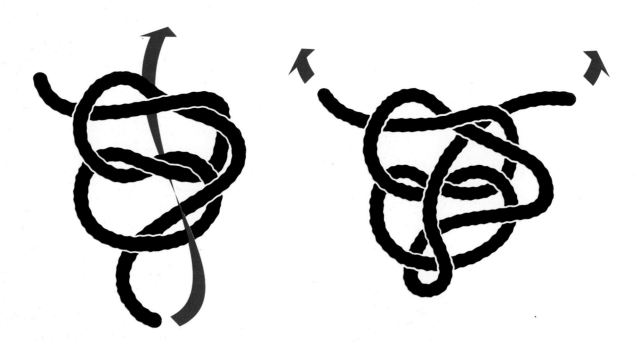

1.

2.

3.

4.

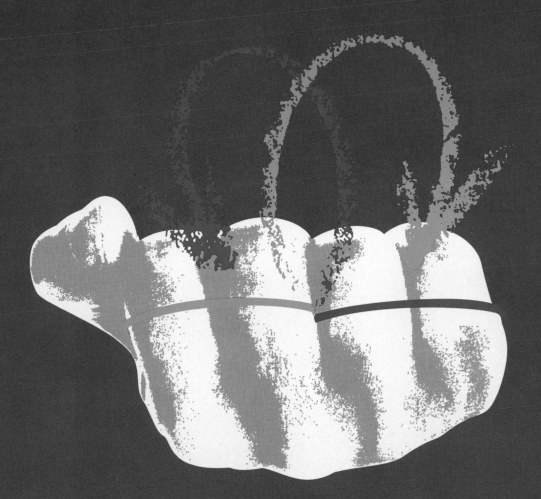

CHANGING BANDS

Make two rubber bands of different colours change places on your fingers. Choose fairly large rubber bands that are slightly loose on your fingers. Pull the bands from the back with the thumb and forefinger of the other hand, and close your hand before the bands snap back, making sure that all four fingers are inside both bands.

From the front it still looks as though the bands are in their original places. Now open your hand and, hey presto, the bands will change places snapping quickly around their adjoining fingers.

The grey in the yellow square looks darker than the grey in the blue square. They are the same - an example of the effect known as colour assimilation.

Tilted into a diamond shape, squares always look larger. These are actually both the same size.

Yes, the long slanting lines
are parallel.

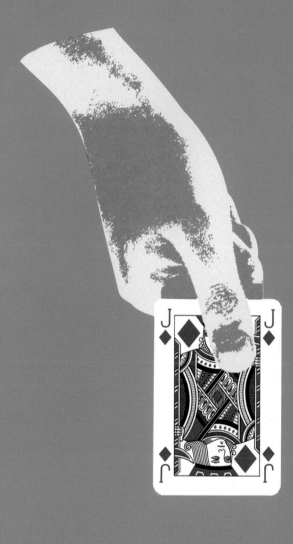

COPYCARD

Take a pack of cards. Give another identical pack to an 'assistant', and tell him to copy everything you do, step-by-step.

1. Shuffle the pack.
2. Exchange packs.
3. Shuffle the pack again.
4. Exchange packs again.
5. Select any card, look at it and put it on top of the pack.
6. Cut the pack.
7. Exchange packs again.
8. Look through the cards, remove the selected card and hold it face down.
9. Ask your assistant to turn up his card. Then amaze him as you turn up your card: it's the same.

The trick is simple. All you have to do is, when you shuffle the assistant's pack at step 3. note the top or bottom card as you hand it back to him to select a card at step 5. The card you have noted is the key card. Cutting the pack at step 6. brings his selected card above or below the key card. His cards come back to you at step 7. Now you know which card your assistant selected, because it is next to the key card you noted. So you remove that one at step 8. and not the one you originally selected.

PENCIL SET

Slowly bring the page up to your face and the two halves of the broken pencil will join.

Despite appearances these
rows of white tiles are
perfectly even. Place a ruler
along the rows to prove it.

THE FLOPPY PENCIL

Take an ordinary pencil and hold it loosely between finger and thumb, a little off centre. Watch as you move your hand up and down (don't move the finger and thumb) and the pencil loses all its rigidity.

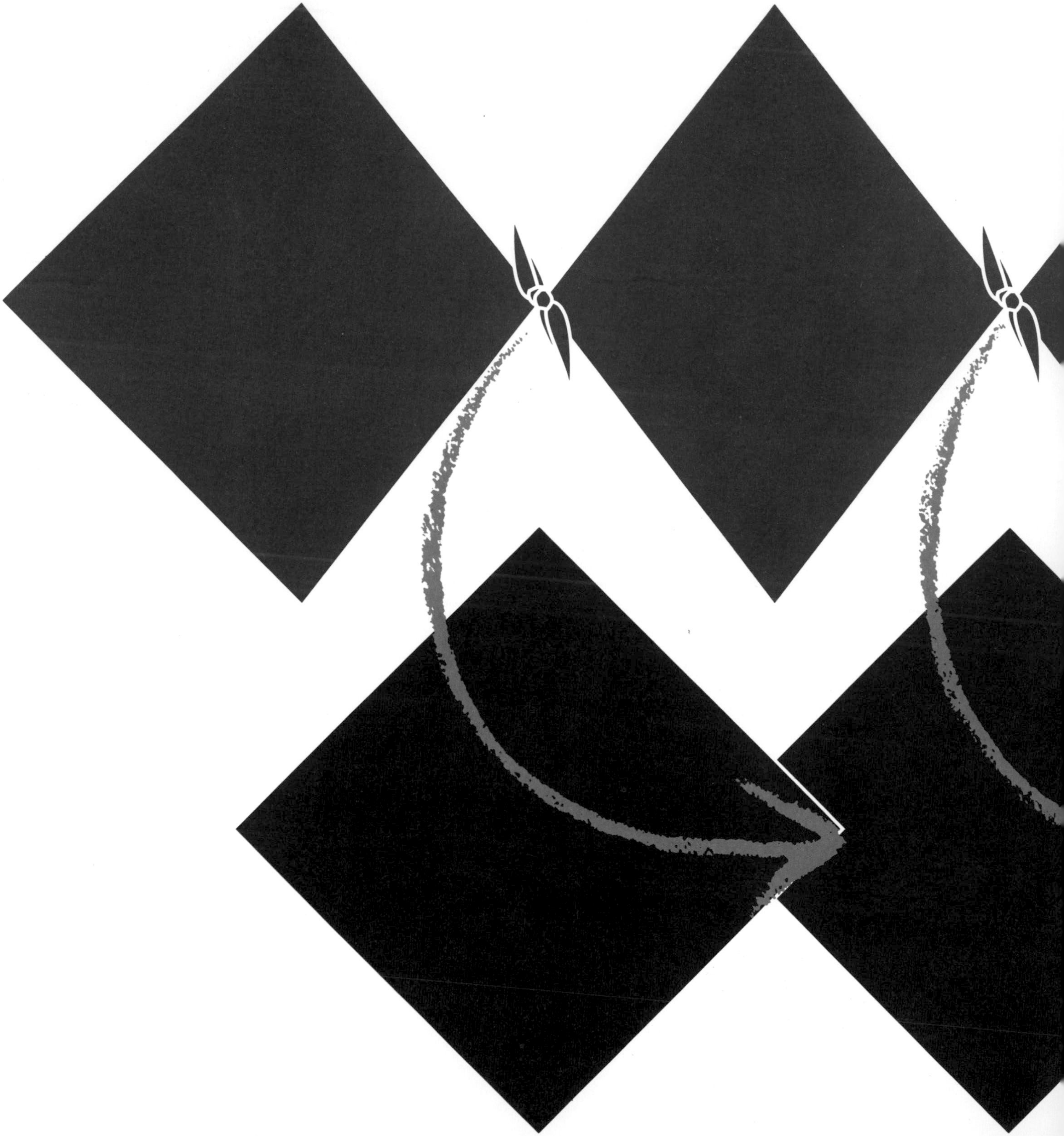

SYMPATHETIC SILKS

Three red silk squares are tied together and three blue silk squares are not. With the appropriate magic words the red silks become untied and the blue silks tied together. The trick is in the preparation. You do in fact tie the blue silks together with tight knots, but to make them appear as three single silks hold them up by the corners next to (not opposite from) the knots. The knots are hidden in the folds.

Now tie the red silks in front of your audience using a special dissolving knot. First twist the ends together and then tie a simple fold-over knot on the top. This looks like a real knot when you are tying it and when it is finished.

Show the audience your silks first as if they were all single. Keep your hands together and count the silks from hand-to-hand so you don't give away the fact that the blue ones are tied. Place the silks over the backs of two chairs. Say the magic words. Pick up the corner of a blue silk and show them all tied together. Then pick up the corners of a red silk and with a shake they all fall apart.

1.

2.

3.

VANISHING MATCHES

Prepare for this trick by pushing a half-full box of matches up your sleeve. (Secure it with a rubber band if your sleeve is very loose.) Now take an empty match-box and shake it. Your audience will think they can hear it rattling with matches, but actually they hear the match-box up your sleeve. Ask them to guess how many matches are in the box you are holding. When you have taken their bids, open it to reveal that it is - empty.

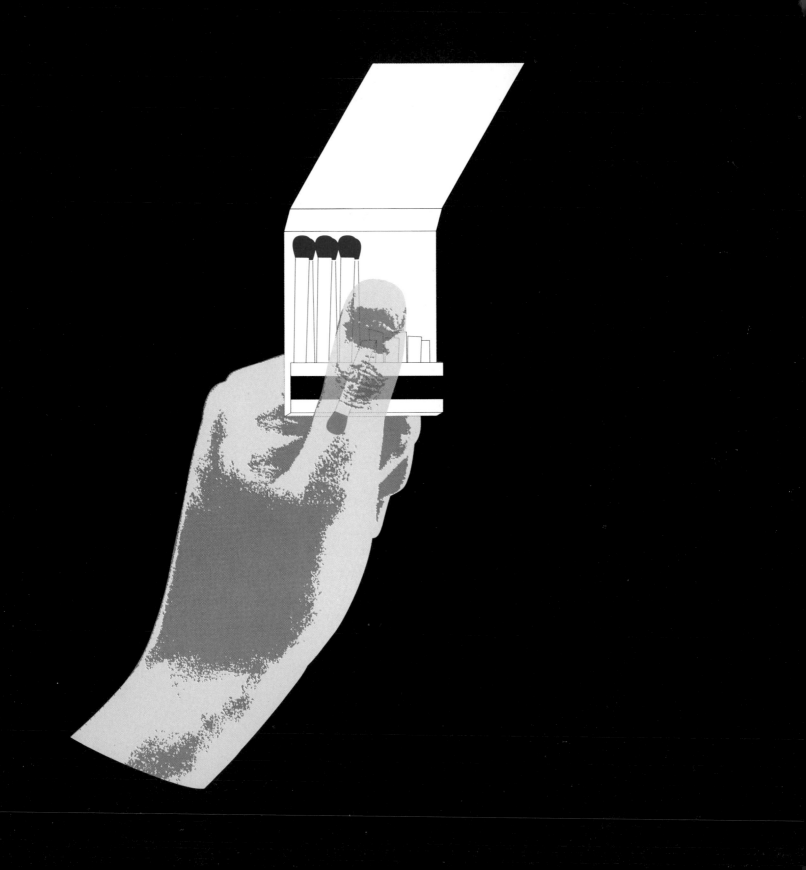

The sides of the square placed on concentric circles appear to be bent. In fact they are straight.

COLOUR SPIN

What colours are hidden in this black-and-white pattern? Take a photocopy of the pattern, glue it to a card and cut it out, with a hole in the middle to take a pencil. Twirl the pattern and you will see colours appear in the spinning bands.

BLONDE ANGLE

Hold the page so you are looking along it from the bottom right hand edge. Who do you see?

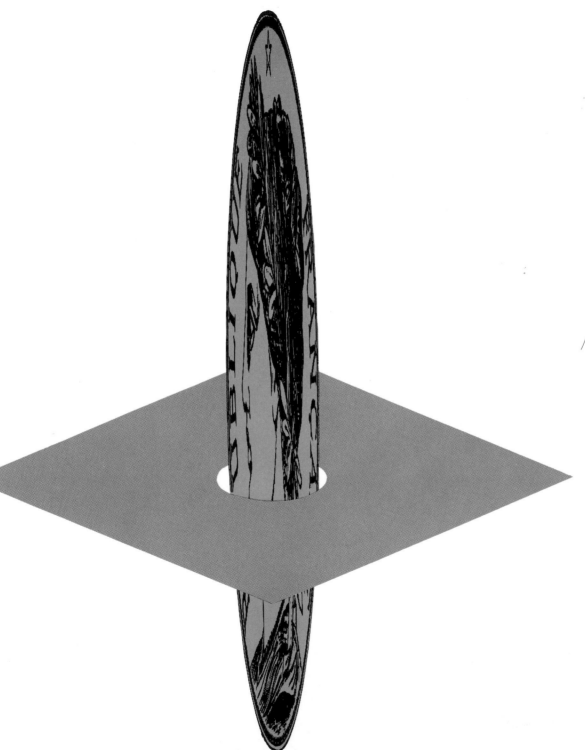

IMPOSSIBLE HOLE

Trace round a small coin on a piece of paper and cut it out. No-one will care much that the coin will pass through the hole. But take a larger coin and promise your audience that you can pass that through the hole as well - without tearing the paper.

What you do is fold the paper across the diameter of the hole, ease the edges of the hole over the larger coin. As it protrudes, bend the folded edges down and the coin will come through.

INNER CIRCLES

The two circles at the centres of the arrangements are the same size.

Roll the flexible mirror that comes with this book into a tube. Place the tube on the circle of the anamorphosis - the name for this specially distorted picture - and it will reveal its hidden reality in the tube mirror. The picture is called *Man with His Stomach in a Wheelbarrow*, an original anamorphosis from the Gold Collection of Toys at the Museum of the City of New York.

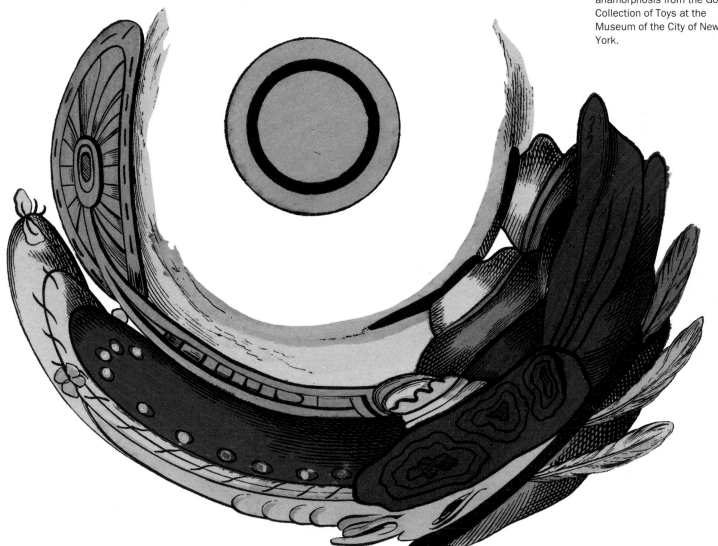

HAT LOSS

The idea is to toss a coin into a hat so that it appears to drop straight through into a waiting glass beneath. The trick is all in the setting up. (You need to be clever here to make sure your audience doesn't see what you're up to - a chance to try the French Drop on page 8.) While placing the hat upturned onto the glass, you slip a hidden coin between the hat and the glass rim so that it is held in place by the weight of the hat.

Now take an identical coin and toss it with some flamboyance into the hat, while secretly just nudging the hat itself. The original coin falls into the glass with a clink; it appears to your audience that the tossed coin has fallen right through the hat.

SPINNING WHEEL

Move the page about at
random and you can see
the wheel turning.

One of these spirals is made
with a single line, one with
two lines. Try and find out
which is which, before
resorting to a pencil.

THE GREAT WHITE

If the white square looks bigger than the black, it is only because darker shapes tend to look smaller than lighter shapes. These two are the same size.

Although the horizontal lines appear to be longer in each successive diagram, they are all the same length.

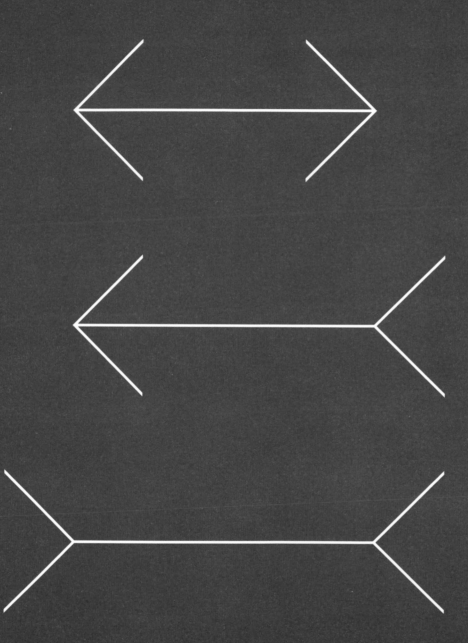

WHERE'S THE CATCH?

Ask two people to hold up a handkerchief; you will need a sturdy one for this trick. Take a safety pin and pin it near the edge with the small end on the top edge and the head of the pin above it. The open side of the pin should be to the right and the solid part to the left, completely over the edge.

Now you can amaze your audience by pulling the pin by the small end to the right along the top of the handkerchief. What you are really doing from the back is folding the material over through the catch of the pin. When you stop moving the pin, it will still be through the handkerchief but the material will be undamaged.

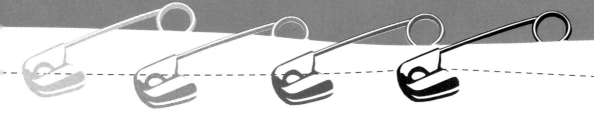

Place a small tube to your right eye. Now hold your left palm towards you against the side of the tube. Look with both eyes into the distance and, rather alarmingly, you can see through a hole that has appeared in your hand.

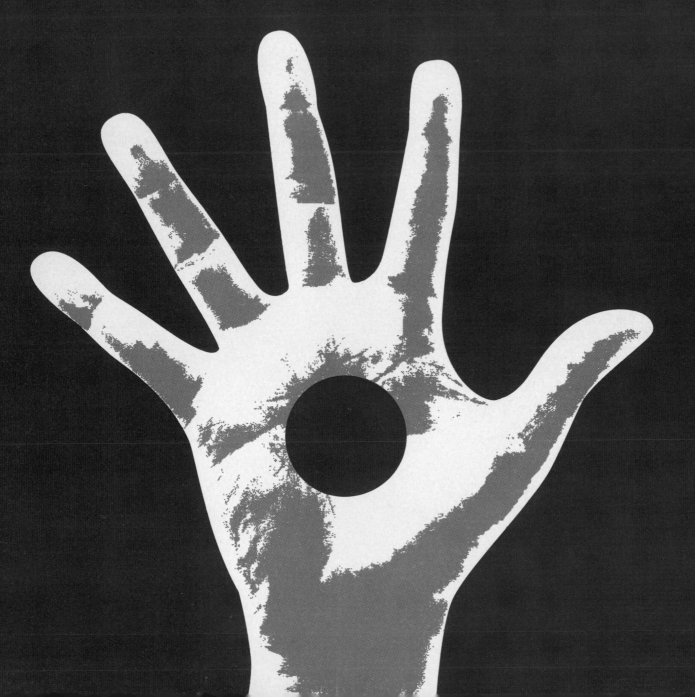

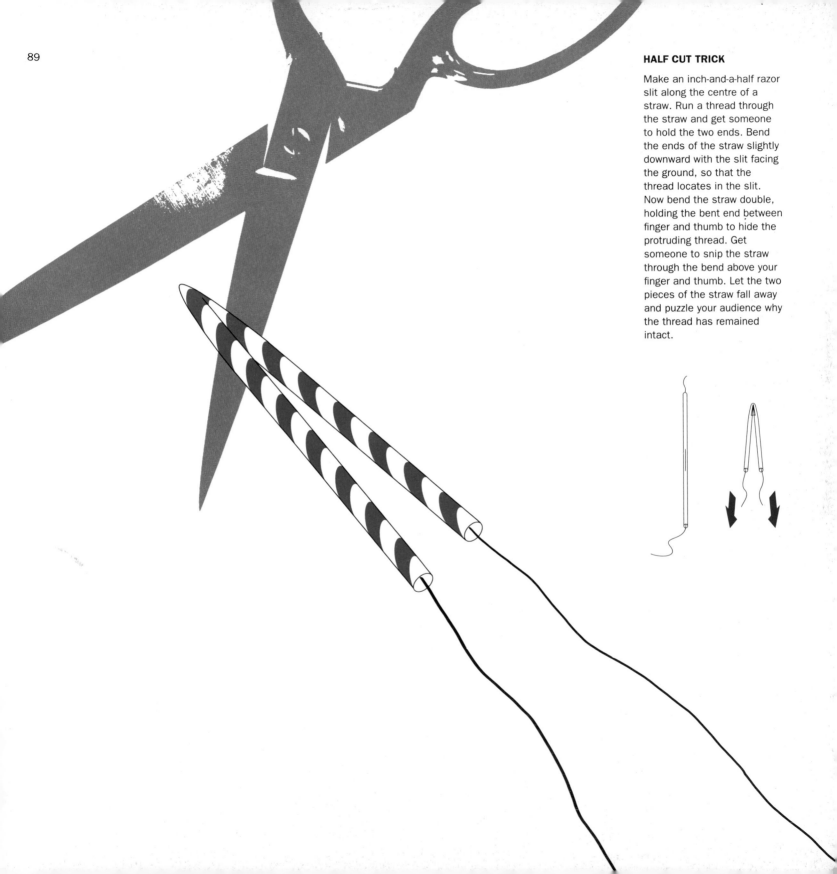

HALF CUT TRICK

Make an inch-and-a-half razor slit along the centre of a straw. Run a thread through the straw and get someone to hold the two ends. Bend the ends of the straw slightly downward with the slit facing the ground, so that the thread locates in the slit. Now bend the straw double, holding the bent end between finger and thumb to hide the protruding thread. Get someone to snip the straw through the bend above your finger and thumb. Let the two pieces of the straw fall away and puzzle your audience why the thread has remained intact.

KNOTS LANDING

Coil a rope and let it drop to the floor. As it drops, it ties itself in knots. This trick depends on how you coil the rope.

1. Hold one end of the rope in your right hand as shown and take up a length of rope in your left hand.

2. Loop the length of rope in your left hand over the right hand as shown.

3. Take another length of rope in your left hand.

4. Loop the second length of rope over the right hand in the same way.

5. Continue like this until the rope is fully coiled. Grip the loose end of the rope by the fingers of your right hand and release the original end you held, letting the coils drop to the floor. As many knots as there were coils will appear in the rope.

1.

2.

3.

4.

5.

STAR STRUCK

Close your right eye. Gradually bring the page closer and closer to your face as you watch the right star. The other two stars will disappear and reappear at different points as you get closer.

(There is a blind spot on the retina at the back of the eye - off-centre where the optical nerve is attached. We only know it's there by doing a trick like this.)

MATCH MENDING

Before you start this trick, hide a wooden match in the seam of a handkerchief. Now take another match, place it in the handkerchief and fold it up. Offer the folded handkerchief to a member of the audience so that they can feel the match you originally concealed. Ask the person to break it. Open the handkerchief and an unbroken match falls out!

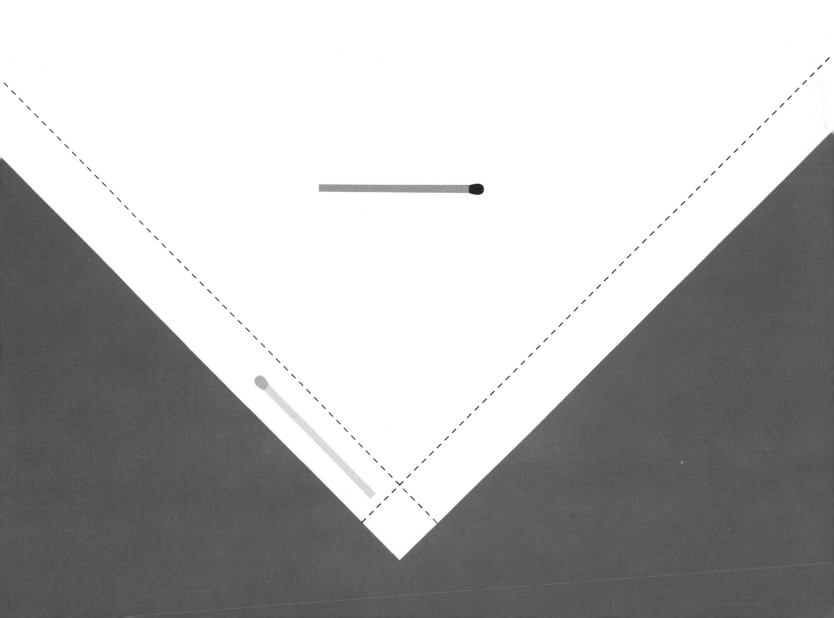

EYE LINES

The two vertical lines here
are the same length. It's
difficult to believe this one
without checking it.

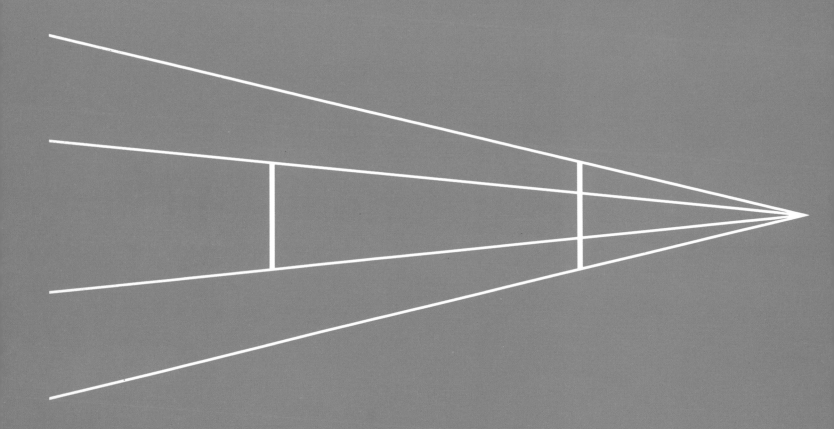

CURVED SQUARE

Close one eye, bring the page close to the other and the checker board loses its distortion and becomes square.

How far can you get walking
up these steps? Give up?
Try walking down again. It's
just as far to the bottom.

THE CRAZY TYPE

In fact these letters are all
quite upright. It's the black
and red overlap outlines that
make them appear tilted.
Only try this when sober.

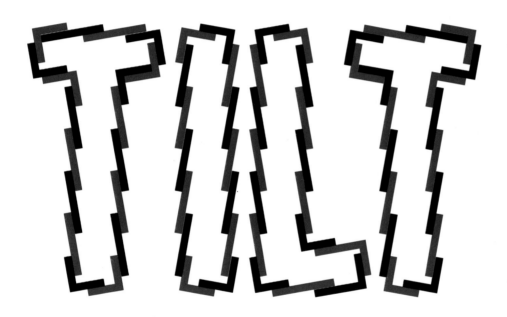

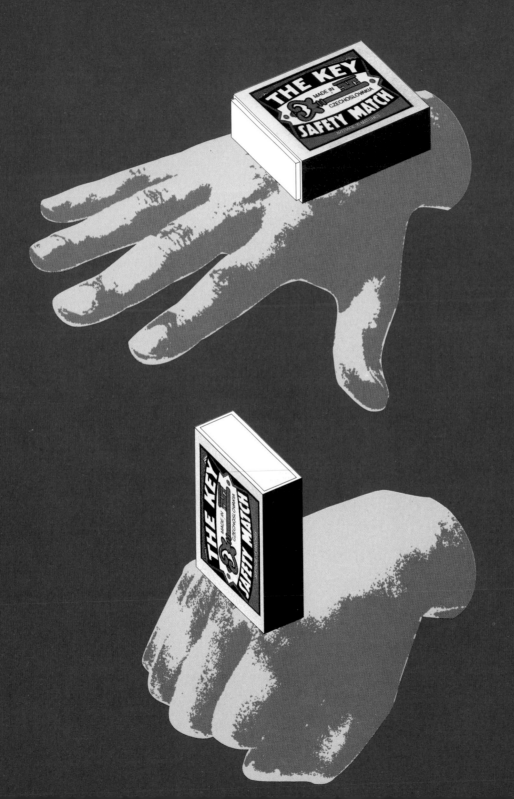

VERTICAL HOLD

Lay a match-box on the back of the hand and make it stand on end without touching it. Ask your audience to try this trick first. While they are finding out it is impossible, secretly prepare your own match-box. The match-box must be empty. Open it a little and lay the open end down on the loose skin of the knuckles. Close the match-box so that it pinches up a little knuckle skin. Now you are ready. When the audience has given up trying to do it, show them your match-box laying on the back of your hand. Close your fist and the match-box sits up on its end. Magic.

Are there six bricks here, or seven? If you take the black as the tops of the bricks there are less than if you take black as the bottoms of the bricks.

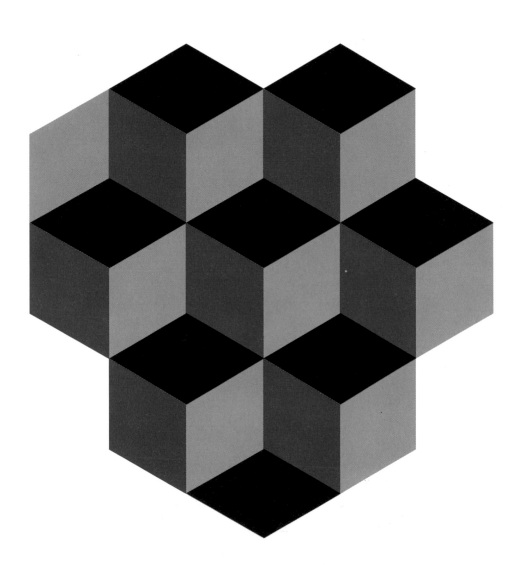

DOTTY FIGURE

There's someone lurking in these dots. If you can't see who it is, try moving the image away from you.

INITIAL ILLUSION

Do you see it? Use your eyes
for a start. (There's a clue in
here somewhere.)

A

B

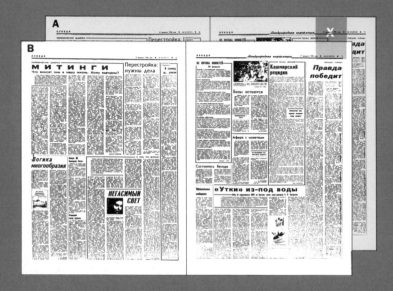

1.

3.

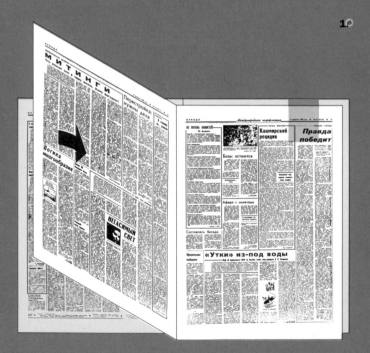

2.

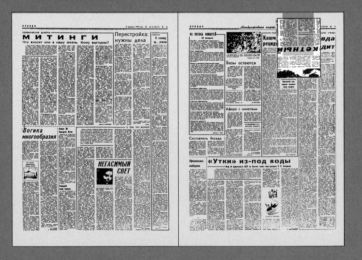

4.

103

5.

SPECIAL EDITION

You can tear a newspaper in half, but can you put it back together again? For this you need the outside pages of two copies of the same edition, unfolded.

Put some paste on the inside of newspaper A at the point marked X.

Lay the newspaper B face up on newspaper A and press on the pasted square (fig 1). Fold the left hand page of newspaper B to the right (fig. 2).

Fold the lower half of newspaper B upwards (fig. 3).

Fold the left hand side of newspaper B to the right again and the lower half upwards again. Continue in this way until newspaper B is in a small 'packet' with the edges folded in and stuck to the back of newspaper A (fig. 4). Complete the preparation by refolding newspaper A with the packet B inside.

Open out newspaper A with the packet B hidden from the audience. Tear newspaper A in half (fig. 5).

Place the back page over the front, and tear in half again. Continue in this way, each time placing the torn pieces in front so that packet B is always kept free at the back (fig. 6-8).

Scrumple the torn pieces into a ball and bring packet B to the front.

Unfold packet B and reveal the 'restored' newspaper (fig. 9), making sure you hold the scrumpled torn pieces safely behind with your hand.

6.

7.

8.

9.

Which building appears to
have the thicker columns?
They are actually the same.

THE CURIOUS CUBE

Can you find where any of
the lines that make up this
diagram meet at right
angles? You wouldn't believe
it at first, but the two inside
angles at the edges of the
beak are in fact 90°.

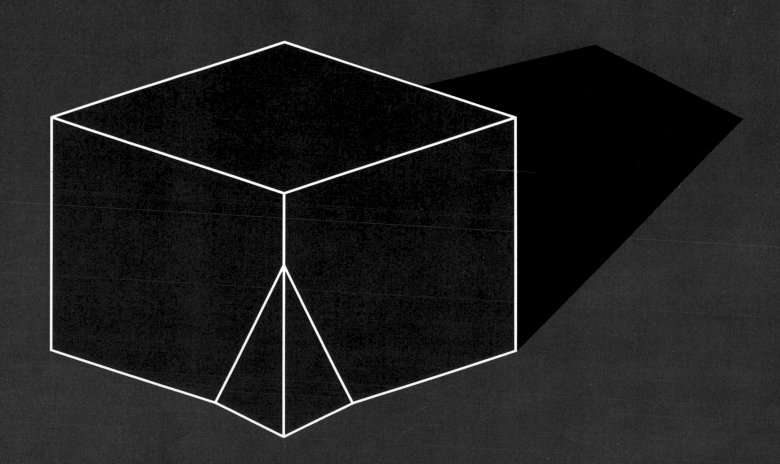

WRONG WAY ROUND

If you place your flexible mirror along the arc and look at the main reflection of the two arrows, you'll see they are now both pointing the same way.

THE MACKAY EFFECT

The perfectly regular repetitive pattern generates curved shadow effects around the centre, although they are not actually in the pattern itself. MacKay was the fellow who first drew this in 1957.

RING UP YOUR PENCIL

Tie a fine thread to the top of a pencil. Tie the other end to something like a button on your shirt. Slip a ring over the pencil and the thread. When you move the pencil away from your body... mysteriously the ring will rise.

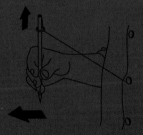

ASCENDANT LINE

Vertical lines usually look
longer than horizontal lines
of the same length.

COLOUR TRANSFERS

Gaze hard for 45 seconds at the cross on the left surrounded by the four coloured segments. Quickly switch your gaze to the solitary cross on the right. You will see four ghostly surrounding segments in colours which are the complements to the ones on the left.

(Suddenly confronted with grey where there was colour before, your eyes 'see' the colours that, if put together with the original colours, would make up grey.)

PARROT-AND-CAGE THAUMATROPE

Take a photocopy of this page. Cut out the two discs and glue them back-to-back on to a cardboard disc the same size. Punch holes at A and B and insert pieces of string through them. Twist up the pieces of string, and when fully wound pull them gently apart so that the disc whirls. The parrot appears to have got into the cage. The effect is called thaumatropic. Try it with other images.

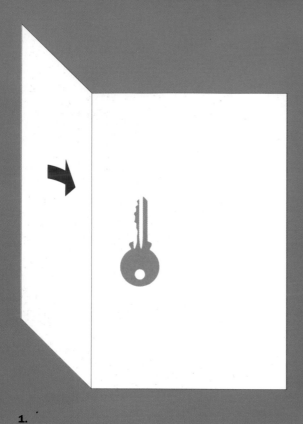

1.

2.

DISAPPEARING KEY

Wrap up a key in a piece of paper. When you unfold the paper the key has gone. Here's how.

1. Place the key on the paper and fold a third over towards you.

2. Turn the paper over so the fold is underneath, and fold the other third towards you.

3. Make another fold of a third upwards making a 'wallet' with the key inside.

4. Turn the 'wallet' over and fold the other third, making sure the key is not trapped in the blind side of the fold.

5. The key now appears well and truly wrapped up in the paper. At this point you can let it slip out and conceal it. Open the paper and the key has disappeared.

3.

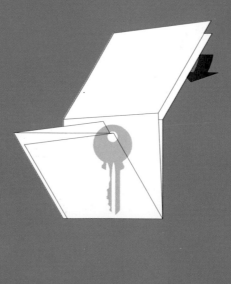

4.

5.

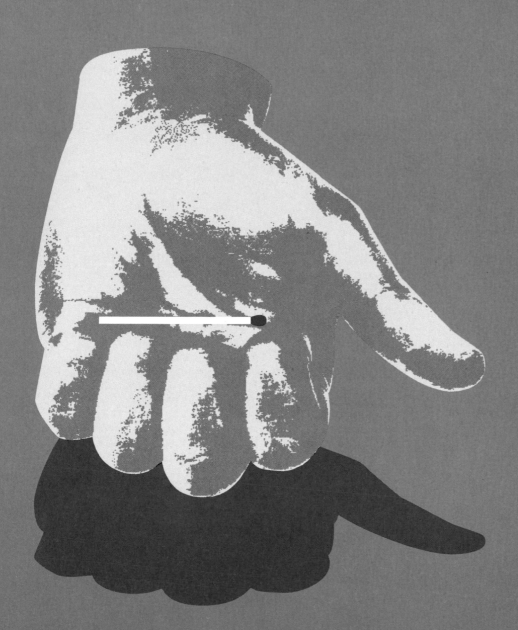

MYSTERY MATCH

Open both hands flat. Ask someone to lay two matches, one in each palm. Now close your fingers and ask the person to lay two more matches one across each row of fingertips. Quickly turn both hands over and pretend to fumble, dropping two matches on the floor. What you have really done is let both matches from one hand fall, while the other hand is quickly opened and closed so the fingertip match drops inside to join the palm match.

Tell your audience the matches slipped the first time and ask for the two fallen matches to be replaced on the fingertips as before. Now turn over the hands again, but this time open and close both quickly so the fingertip matches join the palm matches in each hand. When you open your hands there are three matches in one and one in the other - as if one had mysteriously changed hands.

The stripes in both circles are exactly horizontal, although they appear to slope towards the centre.

BREAKING THE LINE

When a line crosses a grating
of parallel lines at an angle
of less than 45°, the line
seems to break up.

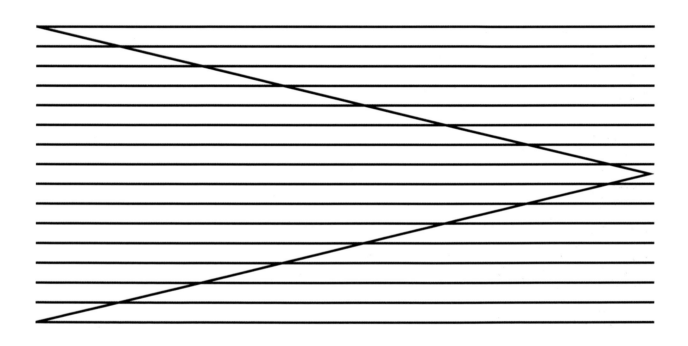

Gaze at the green lips of
Marilyn for about half a
minute. Quickly shift your
eyes to the white paper and
you can see an image of
those lips in their true colour.

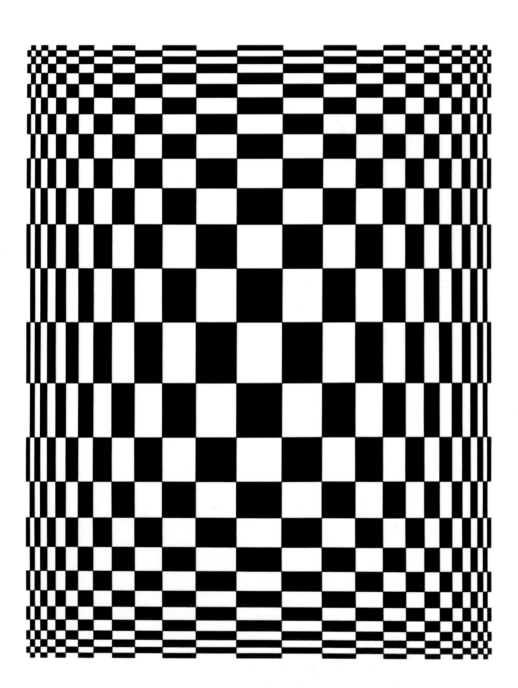

CURVED FLAT

This pattern is made up from nothing but straight-sided rectangles. Yet it has a curved, three-dimensional appearance.

CUT AND RESTORE THE TWINE

Take a piece of two-ply parcel twine about 18 inches long. Separate the strands from the centre, and pull them out as shown. Twist the strands together so that they look like the ends of the twine. Now separate the real ends by a couple of inches. Cut back one strand from each end and twist the uncut ends together using some wax or glue to keep them in place. Finally, tie a knot where the fake ends start, and you have what appears to be a piece of twine tied in a loop. Ask a spectator to cut across the loop with a pair of scissors (which gets rid of the glued part). Untie the knot, tug on the cut ends - and the twine is restored to a single length.

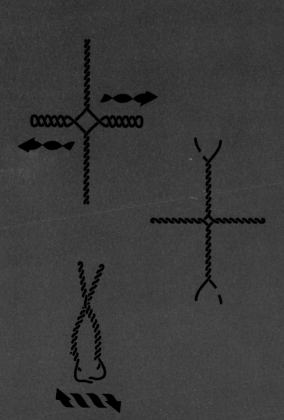

MORE ANAMORPHOSIS

Roll the flexible mirror that comes with this book into a tube. Place the tube on the circle of the anamorphosis - the name for this specially distorted picture - and it will reveal its hidden reality in the tube mirror. The picture is called *Puss-in-Boots*, an original anamorphosis from the Gold Collection of Toys at the Museum of the City of New York.

123

ALL SHAPES AND SIZES

Different angles and different shapes make these figures seem to be different sizes. In fact, they all have exactly the same area.

THE CARD BALANCE

Appear to stand a glass on a playing card. The trick is to have a double card with half of the back card bent to form a stand. Don't let anyone round the back though.

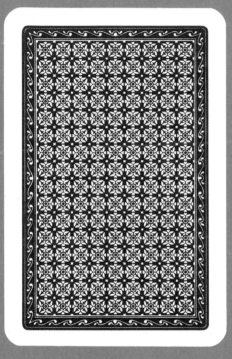

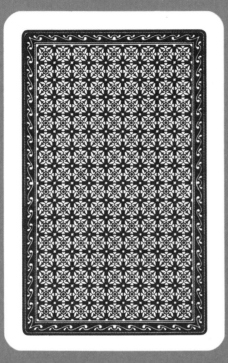

RED AND BLACK DIVISION

Mystify a spectator by dealing out a pack of cards face down, and asking him to guess whether each card may be a red or a black. As he calls the red cards, deal those into one pile and as he calls black cards, deal those into another. Half way through the pack, declare that you are going to reverse the piles. Complete the dealing and turn the cards over. Sure enough, each pile is divided into reds and blacks!

What you have done is prepare the pack so that the first half you deal is all reds. At the point where you reverse the piles - confusing the spectator - you have two red piles; the rest of the cards are all black. So you end up with two piles, both with blacks and reds separated.

Rotate the page rapidly in an anti-clockwise direction and around the centre of the pattern you will see a strange and perfect grey disc appear from nowhere.

STAR SIGN

It may look as though a star
has been superimposed on
the circles, but it isn't really
there at all.

The four planks seem to be bent and bowed. It's an illusion; they are all straight and parallel. The hatching patterns make them seem out of true.

Look at an object through an empty glass. Fill the glass with water and look again. The object has turned back to front.

THE GREAT THUMB ESCAPE

You will need a piece of string, about a foot long, and an assistant.

1. Hang the string over your right thumb from the centre and ask your assistant to tie the string to your right thumb with the knot on top. Arrange the ends A and B so that they hang down either side of the hand.

2. Place your left thumb against the string A hanging down the outside of your right hand, as shown.

3. Bring the left thumb up with the string A and place it on top of the knot on your right thumb.

4. Ask your assistant to tie a knot on top of your left thumb so the two thumbs seem to be tied securely together.

Now you are ready to amaze your audience - including your assistant. Ask him whether he tied the knots good and tight on both thumbs. When he says yes, move your right thumb on top of your left thumb, and left thumb can easily escape.

1.

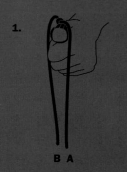

B A

2.

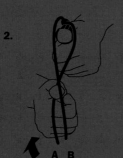

A B

3.

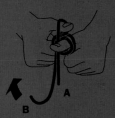

B A

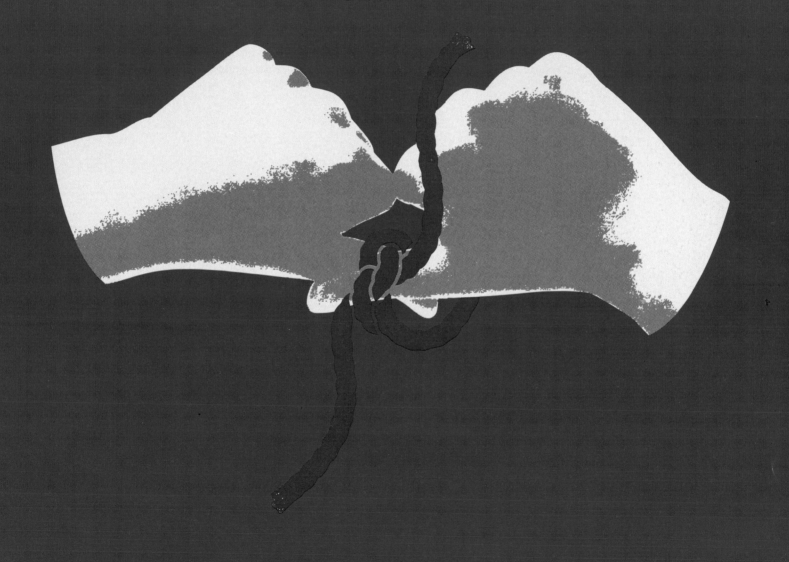

134

PLANK CHECK

How many planks are there? Count the number along the bottom. Count the number along the top.

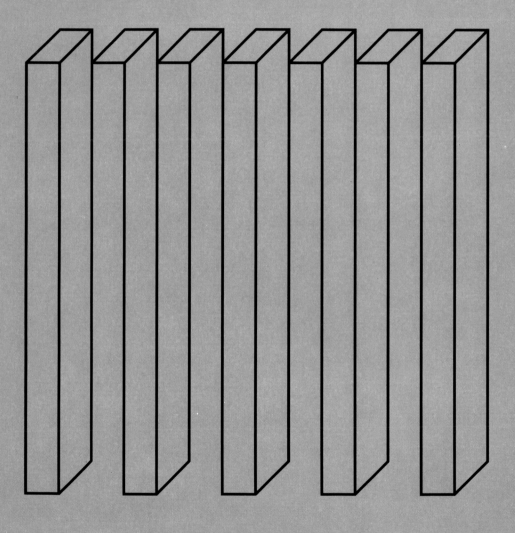

There is only one red and one blue on this page, although they appear as different hues. The effect, known as colour assimilation, changes the appearance of colours depending on what colours they are associated with.

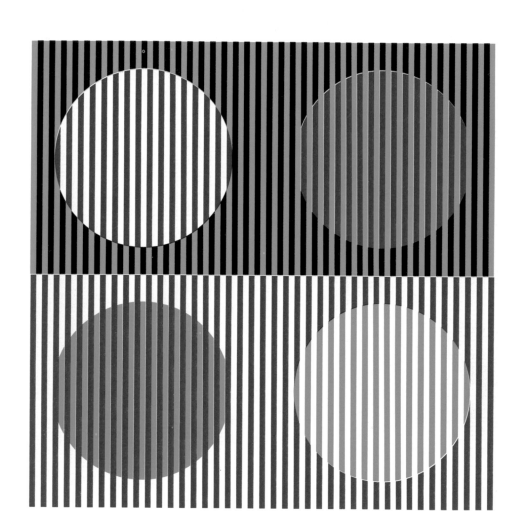

A perfect circle placed on two chevrons of different angles takes on quite an imperfect look.

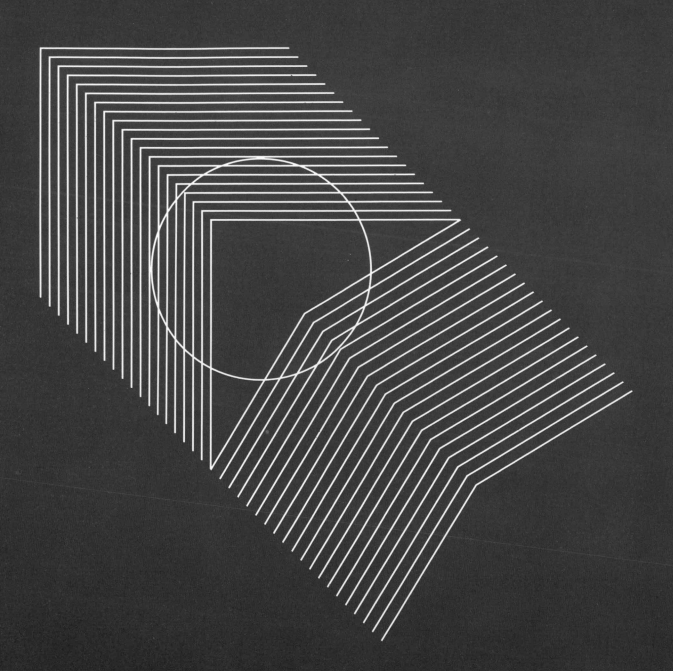

YET MORE ANAMORPHOSIS

Roll the flexible mirror that comes with this book into a tube. Place the tube on the circle of the anamorphosis - the name for this specially distorted picture - and it will reveal its hidden reality in the tube mirror. The picture is called *The Ballet Dancer*, an original anamorphosis from the Gold Collection of Toys at the Museum of the City of New York.

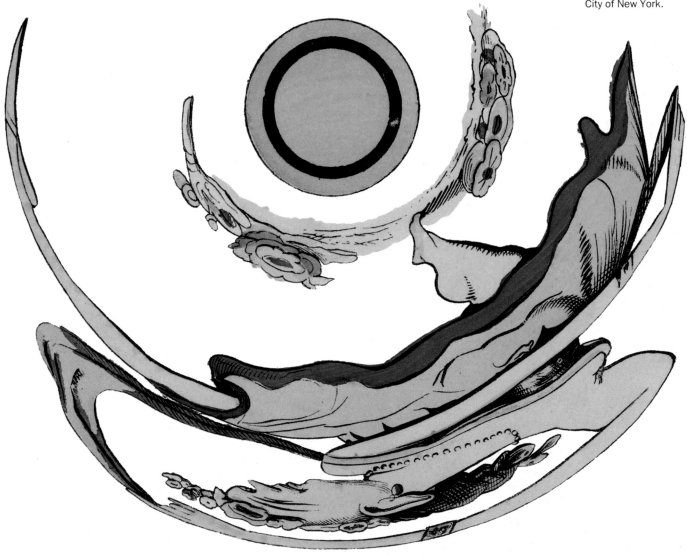

138

COUNTRY PURSUITS

Can you find out which countries these flags belong to? They are shown here not in their true colours, but in their complementary colours. To discover how they really should look, stare hard at them for about half a minute; then look quickly at blank white paper. The real colours of the flags appear before your eyes - and you should be able to identify them. (Not necessarily in this order, they are: France, Germany, Sweden, Italy, Spain, Denmark.)

The Canadian flag unwittingly (or not?) contains two faces. Look at the white space above the maple leaf. Two profiles, foreheads together and snarling at each other, are made out of the top left and right edges of the leaf.

1

2

3

4

BOX CLEVER

1. Tie a piece of string around a matchbox cover.

2. Push one end through the tunnel.

3. Slip the knot off the end of the box. Ask someone to hold the ends of the string, one in each hand.

4. Move the box to hide the knot. When the ends are pulled, no knot. Hmmm.

X-RAY ENVELOPE

Ask someone to write a number on a slip of paper and fold it so you can't see it. Now you place this note in an envelope, seal it and set it alight. When the envelope is reduced to ashes you tell your audience what the number was.

You need to prepare the envelope by cutting a slit about two inches long in the front so it can't be seen from the back. Hold up the envelope with the flap open and facing the audience. Take the folded note and place it in the envelope. What the audience doesn't realise is that you have stuck it partially through the slit. Seal the envelope and hold it up to the light so the audience can see the note is still inside.

Now hold the envelope in your left hand and slip the note out through the slit with your thumb. At the same time set light to the envelope with a lighter. As the audience watches the flames, glance at the note and reveal that you know the secret number.

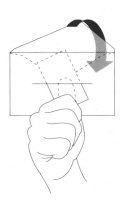

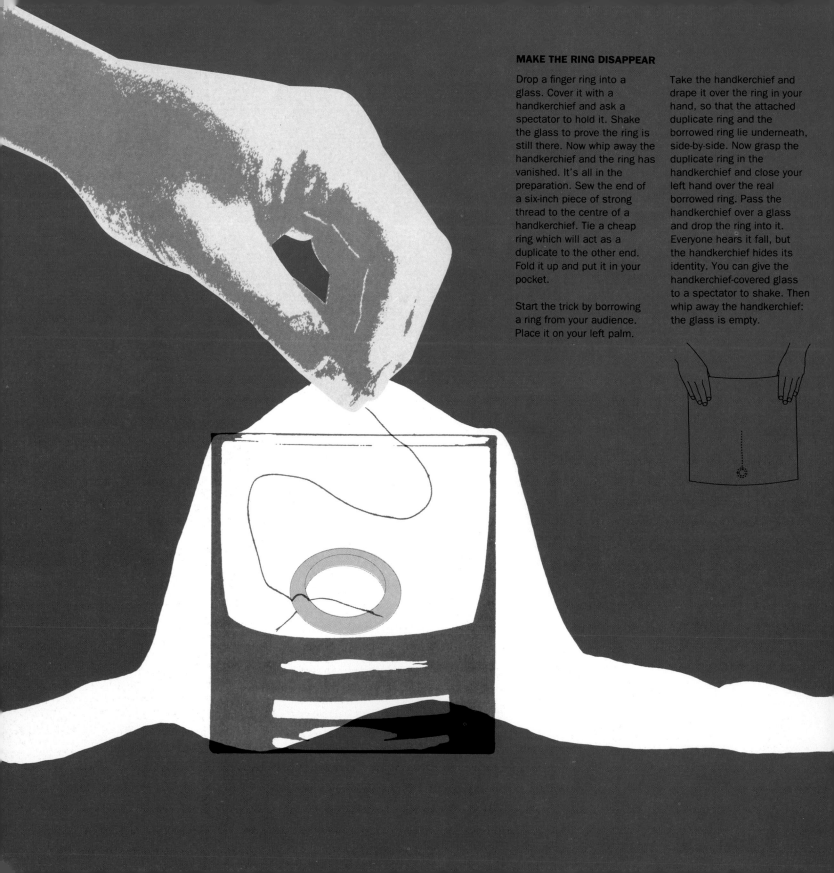

MAKE THE RING DISAPPEAR

Drop a finger ring into a glass. Cover it with a handkerchief and ask a spectator to hold it. Shake the glass to prove the ring is still there. Now whip away the handkerchief and the ring has vanished. It's all in the preparation. Sew the end of a six-inch piece of strong thread to the centre of a handkerchief. Tie a cheap ring which will act as a duplicate to the other end. Fold it up and put it in your pocket.

Start the trick by borrowing a ring from your audience. Place it on your left palm.

Take the handkerchief and drape it over the ring in your hand, so that the attached duplicate ring and the borrowed ring lie underneath, side-by-side. Now grasp the duplicate ring in the handkerchief and close your left hand over the real borrowed ring. Pass the handkerchief over a glass and drop the ring into it. Everyone hears it fall, but the handkerchief hides its identity. You can give the handkerchief-covered glass to a spectator to shake. Then whip away the handkerchief: the glass is empty.

MAKE THE RING REAPPEAR

The trick opposite may worry the owner of the ring. You can be reassuring and make the ring reappear, inside a ball of wool. For this you need a sheet of aluminium or tin about 2 inches by 2¾ inches. Bend it to form a flat tube about ¾ inch wide and 2¾ inches long, so that a ring can slide through it. Push the tube into the centre of a ball of wool. When you have made the ring disappear in the trick opposite, tell the audience that the show is over. While they are not paying attention, slip the ring into the tube, withdraw the tube and put it into your pocket. Announce to the audience that there is, of course, some unfinished business. Give the ball of wool to the owner of the ring and watch his face when he finds what's in the middle.

SALT IT AWAY

Here is a trick for after dinner when your audience may not be too critical. You will need a stiff napkin. Mould the napkin around the salt cellar and then let the salt cellar secretly fall into your lap. Your audience will think it is still in the napkin because they can see its shape. Now clap your hand on to the napkin and squash it flat, producing the salt cellar from under the table as if you had knocked it clear through.

TOUCH CONTROL

Look at these hands. Bring
the page up to your face and
the fingers will touch.

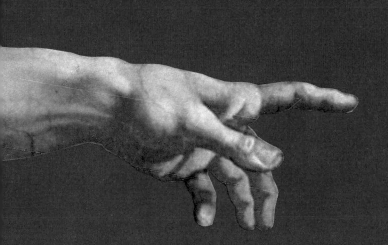
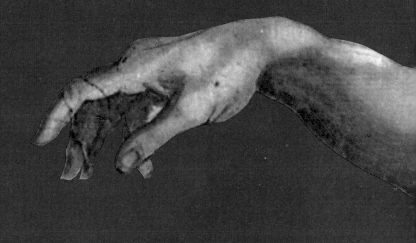

UNSAFETY PINS

Clip two safety pins together. Hold the small end of one pin in your left hand between the thumb and forefinger, with the clip facing upwards. Turn the other pin around the end so that it hangs from the upper bar of the left hand pin, small end at the top - both sides should be over the lower bar and the left side over the upper bar.

The two pins now form and X. Hold the pins tightly and pull them smartly apart as shown. The pin moving to the right slips through the catch of the other pin without forcing it to spring open. Your audience will never see how you did it.

UNCUT THE STRING

Take a piece of thick string about 3 foot long. Cut a 3-inch piece from one end. Loop the small piece and nestle it in your left palm, with the loop towards your fingers. Hold up the large piece of string, one end in each hand. Take the centre of the string in your right hand and place it in your left hand with the ends hanging down. Now pretend to pull the centre of the string through your left fist so that it appears to protrude as a loop. In fact you pull the cut piece out; that is the loop the audience sees. The real centre remains inside the fist held by your third and fourth left fingers; the small piece is held by your thumb and forefinger. Now with your right hand give a pair of scissors to a spectator and ask for the string to be cut in half. Take the scissors back and cut away all the remaining pieces of the protruding string. Hold the string by the ends, one in each hand, and let the centre drop free, showing the string restored.

BY FAR THE LARGER

The figure on the horizon
looks much larger than the
same-sized figure in the
foreground.

149

NEAR AND FAR

Which is the longest line: the green or the red? A trick of perspective; they are both equal.

FAKE FLUSH

By carefully placing two diamond cards on the ace of hearts so that they conceal the lobes of the heart, you can pass off the ace of hearts as an ace of diamonds. A good one for card tricks, but don't try this in a game of poker; you could get yourself shot.

THE GYPSY THREAD

This trick appears to mend a broken thread. Take a length of cotton thread - about a foot long. Crumple half the length into a ball, leaving a little tail. Hide the ball between the thumb and forefinger of your right hand, with the little tail showing. Now break the remaining length of the thread into pieces, holding them prominently in the left hand. Tell your audience that you are magically going to join up the pieces again. Roll the pieces up into a ball - with a little moisture from your mouth. Pretend to 'glue' the ball to the little tail protruding from your right hand, and deftly switch the two balls. With the second ball now hidden between the thumb and forefinger of your right hand, unravel the original ball. An unbroken piece of thread emerges.

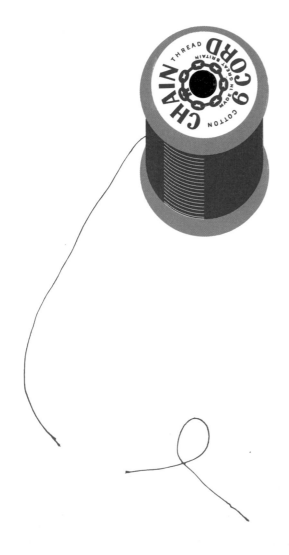

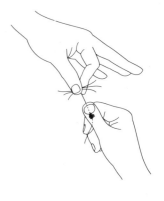

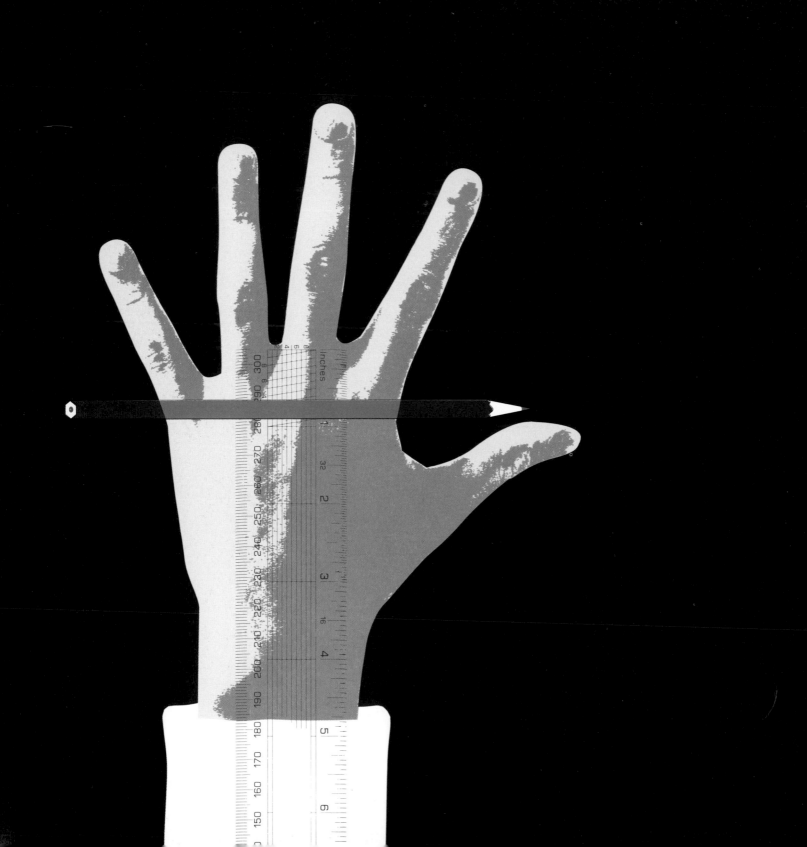

Although the disc nearer the apex of the angle looks larger than the other, they are both exactly the same size.

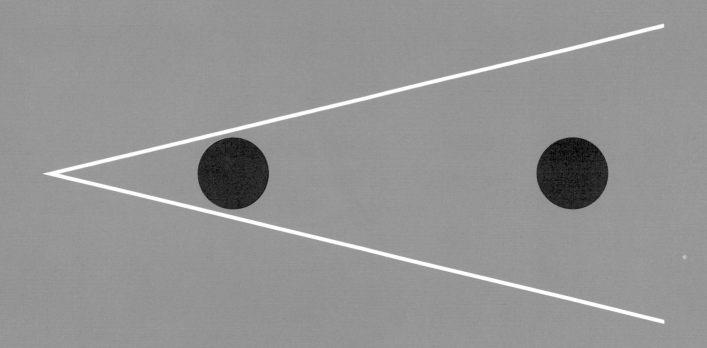

THE IMMATERIAL HANDKERCHIEF

Hold up a coin in your left hand, between fingertips and thumb. With your right hand, spread a handkerchief and drape it over the coin. A spectator can verify the coin is still there by feeling it. Helped by the right hand, the left thumb pinches over a small fold at the base of the coin, at the rear so that it cannot be seen, as shown.

Reassure the audience by giving a brief view of the coin by lifting up the front edge of the handkerchief. Now a deft movement is required. The right hand replaces the handkerchief in front of the coin while the left hand flicks forwards the back half of the handkerchief. Now all the folds of the handkerchief are in front of the coin, as shown.

The coin is now outside and is held horizontally between the middle finger underneath and thumb on top. With the right hand, grasp the handkerchief a few inches below the coin and pull downward as you twist it counterclockwise. Then grip the handkerchief with the second, third and fourth fingers of the right hand while the forefinger and thumb press against opposite edges of the coin. Finally, squeeze the coin into view and show the handkerchief undamaged.

1.

2.

3.

The star is not closer to the top of the triangle than the bottom - it only looks it.

If you tried to make this
pattern out of real blocks,
you might drive yourself
mad. Yet who can say it's
impossible when it is before
your very eyes?

BIBLIOGRAPHY

SOURCES OF REFERENCE

Tricks and Amusements with Coins, Cards, String, Paper and Matches
R M Abraham
Dover Publications Inc (1964)

Colour Perception: A Practical Approach to Colour Theory
Tim Armstrong
Tarquin Publications (1991)

Magic for Beginners
Harry Baron
Kaye & Ward Ltd. (1967)

Modern Coin Magic
J B Bobo
Dover Publications Inc. (1982)

Varied Deceptions
Milbourne Christopher
Supreme

The Illustrated Book of Magic Tricks
Edited by Will Dexter
Abbey Library (1957)

Seeing: Illusion, Brain and Mind
John P Frisby
Oxford University Press (1979)

Mathematical Circus
Martin Gardner
Penguin Books (1981)

Perplexing Puzzles and Tantalizing Teasers/ More Perplexing Puzzles and Tantalizing Teasers
Martin Gardner
Dover Publications Inc (1988)

Illusion in Nature and Art
R L Gregory, E H Gombrich, Colin Blakemore, Jan B Deregowski, H E Hinton & Roland Penrose
Gerald Duckworth & Co (1973)

More Magic
Professor Hoffmann
Martin Breese Ltd. (1988)

Modern Magic Manual
Jean Hugard
Faber & Faber Ltd (1957)

Abbott's Encyclopedia of Rope Tricks for Magicians
Stewart James
Dover Publications Inc. (1975)

Take A Closer Look!
Keith Kay
Bright Interval Books (1988)

Illusions
Edited by Edi Lanners
Holt, Rinehart and Winston (1977)

Hidden Images: Games of Perception, Anamorphic Art, Illusion.
Fred Leeman
Harry N Abrams Inc. (1976)

The Magic Mirror: An Antique Optical Toy
McLoughlin Brothers
Dover Publications Inc. (1979)

Magic and Showmanship
Henning Nelms
Dover Publications Inc. (1969)

Riddles in Mathematics: A Book of Paradoxes
Eugene P Northrop
Penguin Books (1961)

Let's Do Some Magic!
Anthony Parker
The Bodley Head (1956)

The Psychology of Visual Illusion
J O Robinson
Hutchinson University Library (1972)

Practical Sorcery
Alan Shaxon
Goodliffe Publications (1976)

Tricks and Magic
James Webster
Wills & Hepworth Ltd. (1969)